A Manual of
HINDU ASTROLOGY

(CORRECT CASTING OF HOROSCOPES)

Books on Astrology by Dr. B. V. Raman

Astrology for Beginners
A Manual of Hindu Astrology
A Catechism of Astrology
Hindu Predictive Astrology
How to Judge a Horoscope Vol. I
How to Judge a Horoscope Vol. II
Three Hundred Important Combinations
Prasna Marga Vol. I
Prasna Marga Vol. II
Prasna Tantra
Notable Horoscopes
My Experiences in Astrology
Nirayana Tables of Houses
Bhavartha Ratnakara
Ashtakavarga System of Prediction
Graha and Bhava Balas
Hindu Astrology and the West
Planetary Influences on Human Affairs
Muhurta or Electional Astrology
Studies in Jaimini Astrology
Klachakra Dasa
Raman's One Hundred Ten Years Ephemeris (1891-2000)

A Manual of
HINDU ASTROLOGY
(CORRECT CASTING OF HOROSCOPES)

BANGALORE VENKATA RAMAN
Editor, THE ASTROLOGICAL MAGAZINE

UBSPD
UBS Publishers' Distributors Ltd.
New Delhi Bombay Bangalore Madras
Calcutta Patna Kanpur London

UBS Publishers' Distributors Ltd.
5 Ansari Road, New Delhi-110 002
Bombay Bangalore Madras
Calcutta Patna Kanpur London

Copyright © Dr. B.V. Raman

Sixteenth Edition	1992
First Reprint	1993
Second Reprint	1993
Third Reprint	1994
Fourth Reprint	1994

All rights reserved. No part of this publication may be reproduced or transmitted in any form or by any means, electronically or mechanically, including photocopying, recording or any information storage or retrieval system, without prior permission in writing from the publisher or in accordance with the provisions of the Copyright Act 1956 (as amended). Any person who does any unauthorized act in relation to this publication may be liable to criminal prosecution and civil claims for damages.

Printed at Ram Printograph (India), C-114 Okhla Industrial Area, Phase I, New Delhi-110 020

CONTENTS

	Page
Foreword by Prof. B. Suryanarain Rao	xi
Preface to the First Edition	xv
Preface to the Sixteenth Edition	xix
Introduction by Dr. V.V. Ramana Sastrin	xxi
Author's Introduction	xxiii

Chapter I—The Zodiac and the Planetary System

Article		Page
1.	The Zodiac	33
2.	The Ecliptic	33
3.	The Signs of the Zodiac	33
4.	The Constellations	34
5.	The Planetary System	34
6.	Rotation and Revolution	35
7.	Velocities of Planets	36
8.	Retrogression and Acceleration	37

Chapter II—Preliminaries Explained

9.	Rasis and Their Extent	39
10.	Nakshatras and Their Extent	39
11.	Movable Signs	41
12.	Fixed Signs	41
13.	Common Signs	41
14.	Odd Signs	41
15.	Even Signs	42
16.	Signs of Long Ascension	42
17.	Signs of Short Ascension	42
18.	Sirodaya Signs	42
19.	Prustodaya Signs	42
20.	Quadrants	42

Article		page
21.	Trines	43
22.	Succeedent Houses	43
23.	Cadent Houses	43
24.	Oopachayas	43
25.	Planetary Ownerships	43
26.	Exaltation	43
27.	Debilitation	43
28.	Good and Evil Planets	44
29.	Sexes	44
30.	Moolatrikonas	44
31.	Planetary Relations	44
32.	Karakas	45
33.	Bhavas	46
34.	The Astrological Measure	47

Astronomical Terminology

35.	The Axis and Poles of the Earth	47
36.	The Earth's Equator (Vishvarekha)	47
37.	The Latitude (Akshamsa)	48
38.	The Longitude (Rekhamsa)	48
39.	The Celestial Equator (Nadivritta)	48
40.	The Celestial Latitude (Kshepa)	48
41.	The Declination (Kranti)	48

Chapter III—The Ayanamsa

42.	Equinoctial Points	49
43.	Precession of the Equinoxes	49
44.	Movable and Fixed Zodiacs	50
45.	The Sayana and the Nirayana Systems	50
46.	The Ayanamsa	50
47.	Varahamihira's Observations	51
48.	Exact Date of Coincidence not known	51
49.	Use of Ayanamsa	52
50.	Determination of (Approximate) Ayanamsa	53

Article   Page

Chapter IV—Rasimanas

51. Geographic and Geocentric Latitudes ... 55
52. Rasimanas ... 55
53. Charakhandas ... 56
54. Rising Periods on the Equator ... 57
55. Determination of Rasimanas ... 58
56. Duration of Signs in South Latitudes ... 61

Chapter V—Sunrise and Sunset

57. Apparent Time of Rising and Setting of the Sun ... 62
58. Apparent Noon ... 62
59. Ahas and Ratri ... 63
60. Hindu Method of Determination of Sunrise and of Sunset ... 64
61. Modern Method of Determination of Apparent Time of Sunrise and of Sunset ... 69
62. Equation of Time ... 71
63. Method of the Determination of Equation of Time to get Mean Time from Apparent Time ... 71
64. The Mean Time of Sunrise and Sunset ... 74
65. Easy Method of finding the Mean Time of Sunrise and of Sunset ... 75

Chapter VI—Measures and Conversion of Time

66. Hindu Chronology ... 76
67. Local Mean Time ... 78
68. Standard Time ... 80
69. The Standard Horoscope ... 81
70. Suryodayadi Jananakala Ghatikaha ... 81

Chapter VII—Graha Sphutas

71. The Hindu Almanac ... 83
72. Method of Making Graha Sphutas ... 83
73. Nirayana Longitude of Planets ... 86

viii

Article		Page
Chapter VIII—**Lagna Sphuta**		
74. Lagna or Ascendant	...	88
75. Solar Months	...	88
76. Determination of Lagna	...	89
77. Rasi Kundali	...	91
Chapter IX—**Dasama Bhava Sphuta**		
78. The Dasama Bhava	...	92
79. Rasi Chakra	...	92
80. Conception of Bhava Chakra	...	93
81. Bhaskara's Definition	...	93
82. Bhava Chakra	...	94
83. Method of Determination of the Mid-heaven		94
Chapter X—**Bhava Sphutas**		
84. Bhava or House	...	100
85. Bhava Madhyas	...	100
86. Kendra Bhavas	...	100
87. Determination of Kendra Bhavas	...	100
88. Non-Angular Houses	...	101
89. Determination of Bhava Madhyas of Non-angular Houses	...	101
90. Bhava Sandhis	...	105
91. Determination of Bhava Sandhis	...	106
92. Poorva and Uttara Bhagas of Bhavas	...	107
Chapter XI—**Casting the Horoscope according to the Western Method and its Reduction to the Hindu**		
93. General Observations	...	109
94. Hindu and Western Methods	...	110
95. The Modern Ephemeris	...	110
96. Table of Houses	...	111
97. Local Mean Time of Birth	...	111

Article		Page
98.	Greenwich Mean Time of Birth	112
99.	Greenwich Mean Time Interval of Birth	112
100.	Daily Motions of Planets	113
101.	Hindu Nirayana Longitudes of Planets	113
102.	The Sidereal Time of Birth	116
103.	R.A.M.C. at Birth	118
104.	Sayana Longitudes of Angular Houses	118
105.	Nirayana Tables	120

Chapter XII — The Shodasavargas

106.	The Vargas	121
107.	The Varga Divisions	122
108.	The Shadvargas	122
109.	The Saptavargas	122
110.	The Dasavargas	122
111.	The Shodasavargas	123
112.	Rasi	123
113.	Hora	124
114.	Drekkana	125
115.	Chaturthamsa	126
116.	Sapthamsa	127
117.	Navamsa	127
118.	Navamsas and Nakshatra Pada	130
119.	Navamsa Chakra	131
120.	Dasamsa	132
121.	Dwadasamsa	133
122.	Shodasamsa	133
123.	Vimsamsa	134
124.	Chaturvimsamsa	135
125.	Bhamsa	136
126.	Thrimsamsa	137
127.	Khavedamsa	138
128.	Akshavedamsa	139

Article		Page
129.	Shashtyamsa	140
130.	Other Amsas	142
131.	Panchamsa	142
132.	Shashtamsa	142
133.	Ashtamsa	142
134.	Ekadasamsa	143
135.	Nadi Amsa	143
136.	General Remarks	146
137.	Interpretation of Saptavarga Table	147
	Summary	148
TABLE I—Charakhandas (1° to 60° N. Lat.)		156
TABLE II—Terrestrial Latitudes and Longitudes		158
TABLE III—Equation of Time		165
TABLE IV—Table of Standard Times		166
TABLE V—Sunrise and Sunset		175
TABLE VI—Lords of Vargas		179
An Index of Technical Terms		184

SRI

FOREWORD

By
Bangalore Suryanarain Rao

It gives me pleasure to write a few words by way of a Foreword.

The writer of this work, B. V. Raman, is my eldest son's eldest son, *i.e.*, my grandson. I was on the look-out for a competent successor to the special line of researches, *viz.*, astronomico-astrology in which I have spent the major portion on my active life and have found my grandson, a competent youth to take up my work.

He has made an intelligent study of mathematical and predictive astrology and has been able to compose some treatises on this improtant subject.

The necessity of accurate mathematical knowledge is placed beyond a question; and no astrologer of any pretensions can ever hope to become a successful predictor, unless he is competent in his astronomical knowledge of correctly casting the horoscope and finding out the various sources of strength and weakness of the Planets and the Bhavas.

This work, I am proud to say, has been done by my grandson, with considerable skill and ability. He has put his ideas in a flowing, convincing and easy style and the illustrations, he has given, will be found to be of immense use to the readers.

I have been, during the last 60 years of my activities in the astrological line, dealing more or less with the judicial portion of astrology, and have not given as much attention as the subject of mathematical calculations demands. Probably fate ordained, that, while I have fully treated in my own inimitable style the predictive portions, the mathematical portions should be reserved to be elaborated by my own grandson, adding a feather to the line of my succession.

As this book deals with the essential aspects of Mathematical Astrology necessary for correct computation of horoscopes according to the Hindu system, the selection of the name as "A Manual of Hindu Astrology" is quite appropriate.

There has been a very great demand for such a book and I am proud to say that my grandson B. V. Raman has supplied the want with credit to himself.

This book is written with a view to help all those, who are attempting to grasp the fundamental principles of Hindu astronomico-astrology.

To write a book on the mathematical portion requires patience, diligence and devotion, all of which my grandson has displayed in a commendable manner.

I pray God earnestly that he may live to a long age, as God has been pleased to give me longevity, and do as much service to the public as possible. I bless him with all my heart and pray God to make him successful and prosperous.

BANGALORE
5th October 1935 B. SURYANARAIN RAO

PREFACE TO FIRST EDITION

Last year I wrote a comprehensive book entitled *Hindu Predictive Astrology*, the major portion of which has been devoted to the exposition of the predictive branch of the science. But later on, I realised the need for a book devoted to the mathematical side of the subject too, by the constant pressure brought to bear upon me by students of astrology. In casting horoscopes according to approved rules of Hindu Astrology, nothing but a series of mathematical calculations is involved; and hence the present manual is devoted to the exposition of the important and essential principles of Hindu Mathematical Astrology. The mathematical portions dealt with in these pages are very necessary for a student of astrology who wishes to become a successful predictor of future events. *Graha and Bhava Balas* which deals with the method of determination of strengths of planets and houses forms a companion volume to this and a study of both these books will simplify the whole range of astrological mathematics of the Hindus and will enable the student to prepare a suitable ground for venturing predictions. It is hoped the present work will supply a long-felt want. All unnecessary and superfluous information constantly employed by writers on Mathematical Astrology, which are not only cumbersome but also unimportant from the point of view of correct predictions, has been omitted. Ignorance of even the elementary principles of Mathematical Astrology is sure to lead one to the obvious misconception of the fundamental postulates of the judicial system and, at the same time, too much indulgence in mathematics alone is equally harmful as completely atrophying one's judgement faculty and power of induction. Hence to cast and read a horoscope, a moderate knowledge of Mathematical Astrology would be simply invaluable.

This book deals with such aspects as the determination of the longitudes of planets, house-cusps, sunrise and sunset and other information essential for constructing a horoscope.

A separate chapter, exclusively devoted to describing the method of casting the horoscope, etc., accroding to the Western system and its reduction to the Hindu, has been included and this is sure to enhance the value of the book by making it accessible to the Eastern and Western students alike.

The book is intended both for the beginner and the advanced.

The book may have its own defects, and any suggestions for its improvement will be gratefully appreciated.

Original books on *Varshaphal (Annual Reading of Horoscopes) based on Tajaka, Kalachakra Dasas, etc., are in the course of preparation and they will be released for publication in due course, for the benefit of the astrological public. I am specially indebted to my grandfather Prof. B. Suryanarain Rao, to whom this work is dedicated for his valuable instructions to me in Astrology.

I have relied to some extent on the English translation of *Sripathi Paddhati* by Mr. V. S. Subrahmanya Sastri for information on Dasamabhava Sphuta and my thanks are due to him.

I feel certain that my humble endeavours in expounding Astrology will be appreciated by all well-wishers of knowledge and understanding.

BANGALORE
5th October 1935

B. V. RAMAN

---

* *Varshaphal* or *The Hindu Progressed Horoscope* has already undergone eleven editions and is priced Rs. 15-00.

PREFACE TO SIXTEENTH EDITION

I am happy to place before my readers the sixteenth edition of A MANUAL OF HINDU ASTROLOGY.

In this book the reader is provided with all the information needed to construct a horoscope accurately.

A MANUAL OF HINDU ASTROLOGY, NIRAYANA TABLES OF HOUSES and 110-YEAR EPHEMERIS form the essential tools of a student of Astrology for the scientific construction of a horoscope.

The Table of Standard Times has been further revised and updated.

Tables V and VI are indispensable in not only determining sunrise and sunset times but also for the calculation of Vargas or divisions referred to in Chapter XII.

I am thankful to the esteemed public for the continuous encouragement that is being given to my writings on Astrology. I shall feel amply rewarded if by a study of this book my readers are inspired to take a more sustained interest in Astrology and try to master its techniques.

I thank the UBS Publishers' Distributors Ltd., New Delhi, for bringing out this attractive edition.

Dr. B. V. Raman

"Sri Rajeswari"
Bangalore
1st February, 1992

AN INTRODUCTION

By

Dr. V. V. Ramana Sastrin, M.A., Ph.D., F.Z.S., etc.

I am asked to write a few words by way of introduction, which I do with extreme pleasure, even in the face of poor health.

The present volume is devoted to the astronomical basis of Hindu Astrology, not without occasional sidelights on the theory of Western Astrology, but the manner in which the relevant findings are marshalled, and the methods expounded will not fail to hold the attention of the reader.

To the beginner with the merest acquaintance with the astronomical preliminaries, the presentation is bound to make a fascinating appeal, but to the trained student, the book, as a whole, cannot but serve the purpose of a stimulating repertory of the leading facts or concepts of astrological mathematics.

The Author, Prof. B. V. Raman, has already made his mark in the astrological world, and bids fair to hold his own in the future, as a first-rate expounder of Hindu Astrology. He is none other than the grandson of Prof. B. Suryanarain Rao, the venerable doyen of Indian Astrologers of repute, whose personal teaching and example have gone not a little to make of the grandson what he is.

This book is intended to be the first of a series, planned to embrace the several departments of astrology, one after another, and I sincerely bid him God-speed in the successful materialisation of his plans.

VEDARANYAM
TANJORE,
25th September, 1935

V. V. RAMANAN

AUTHOR'S INTRODUCTION

The mathematical basis of astrology is so precise and exact that even its greatest enemies cannot but be convinced of its scientific nature. The noble art of prediction assumes a fair amount or knowledge in the mathematical part of astrology. It cannot be denied that such an ability imposes a great strain on the limited mental acumen of the average astrologer, that his pretensions to make correct predictions are really baseless. It would be better to draw a distinction between mathematical astrology and astronomy. By the former, we mean, the relation of mathematics to astrology in so far as it is concerned with the correct determination of the longitudes of the planets on the basis of reliable ephemerides or almanacs, cusps of the various houses, the different kinds of Balas or sources of strength and weakness of each planet and house, and such other details which are ascertainable with the aid of mathematics so that a sound basis for making correct predictions may be obtained. In other words, mathematical astrology deals with nothing but correct casting of horoscopes. And we classify the methods of computing the longitudes of planets independently, determining the periods of eclipses and such other details as the measurement of the dimensions of the various celestial bodies and their internal and external peculiarities, etc., under astronomy. The ancient Hindus always regarded astrology and astronomy as synonymous so that a bad astronomer was also considered a bad astrologer. In fact the qualifications laid down by great and illustrious writers like Varahamihira and Bhaskaracharya are so rigorous, that we fear that none of us today would be deemed to be called an astrologer at all. Bhaskara stresses on the need for a clear knowledge of spherical astronomy for one, who wishes to be an astrologer and a comprehension of the doctrine of spherical projection and allied theories for locating the true position of planets, etc. But, for our purpose, we shall maintain this distinction, we have called attention to above, in regard to mathematical astrology and astronomy and deem that a fair acquintance with the principles of mathematical astrology is absolutely essential for successful predictions.

A noteworthy sign of this century seems to be a general awakening in the minds of the educated classes to institute a scientific inquiry into ancient subjects like astrology and astronomy. It is, however, deplorable to note that, in their over-enthusiasm to benefit the cause of the science, many of the English educated Indians of today have been adopting an undesirable attitude towards Hindu astronomical calculations in rejecting them altogether as incorrect or inconsistent and replacing them entirely by modern ones, as being quite accurate and precise. The arguments advanced by them, in favour of such a theory, are generally unsound and cannot stand the test of actual demonstration. Are we to reject the Hindu astronomical calculations formulated and adopted by such celebrated exponents of the celestial science as Varahamihira, Bhaskara, Sripathi and others, because they seem to clash with modern ones, while accepting the ancient astrological principles ? A Varahamihira or a Kalidasa who has bequeathed to us such masterpieces as *Brihat Jataka* and *Uttara Kalamritha* could not have been so ignorant or indifferent as to give room for such fallacies, inconsistencies and errors which we are trying to find out in their writings. I would be the height of folly and absurdity to estimate their conclusions in matters of astronomy and astrology in the light of our own developments or achievements in those branches of knowledge. Modern decisions and conclusions cannot be taken as criteria for judging the accuracy or otherwise of the ancient Hindu Astronomers. The extreme accuracy and precision to which we lay claim are oftentimes questionable. It is true that no satisfactory agreement could be found between the writings of any two people even in ancient books. But what of it? Do all modern calculations tally with each other ? Certainly not. Take for instance the measurement of terrestrial latitudes. Each reference book, an authority in its own way, differs decidedly from the other. Bangalore is located on 13°, 12°, 57' and 12° 51" N. Lat.; which of these is correct? Therefore it is useless to reject the ancient methods of calculations completely, because they seem to clash with ours and replace them entirely by those of modern times.

Most of the theories of today are simply tentative; they have not, as yet, been established. The statements of some of the astronomers are really ludicrous and exite sympathy in the hearts of sober men for such perverted views. Modern calculations alone cannot be accepted as correct or accurate (for astrological purpose) and the ancient ones rejected. Moreover the ancient Hindu astronomers dreaded secular interference in matters of astronomy for *astrological purposes*.

The ancient Maharishis were past masters of the first magnitude in almost all branches of knowledge. That they discovered many phenomena by mere observation alone cannot be vouchsafed. The plane of observation employed by them was certainly quite different from that of the modern scientists. The art of Yoga was peculiar to them. Not being satisfied with the nature of the phenomena revealed by glasses and other material objects, they dived deep into the unfathomable depths of Yoga by means of which they were able to see things in their reality, face to face. The first *Sutra* in the *Grahanirnaya Prakarana* of the *Bhoutika Sutras* is "*Darpanemithya Vadaha*" meaning that objects at a distance, viewed through glasses, always present forms, which really do not represent their true state of nature. This clearly suggests, that to get at truth, so far as the celestial and distant objects are concerned, we must view them by something other than glasses, as there are many media between them and earth, whose refracting and dispersing powers, we do not know much about. Thus they had the gift of Yoga, the fragments of which we see even unto this day, which helped them to a great extent in their expeditions in unveiling the mysteries surrounding the phenomenon of the celestial bodies.

There may be still other causes for the existence of differences between modern and ancient astronomical observations. For instance the equation of the Sun's centre according to the Indian tables is $2° 10\frac{1}{2}'$ whereas according to modern observations it is only $1° 55\frac{1}{2}'$. Is the first figure wrong because it differs from the second? It cannot be; for "the eccentricity of the solar orbit on which the equation just mentioned depends was greater in former ages than it is at the present time because of the consequence of natural disturbances of planets". Hindu calculations require consideration of Hindu figures and tables and we have to consider Hindu methods alone in matters of Hindu Astronomy. Prof. Wilson observes that "the science of astronomy at present exhibits many proofs of accurate observation and deduction, highly creditable to the science of the Hindu Astronomers". Take for instance eclipses.

The Hindu methods yield as correct results as the modern methods.

The sciences of Hindu Astronomy and Astrology have got into disrepute by the ignorance of some astrologers whose mercenary nature makes them impervious and indifferent to the grave responsibilities that lie on their heads; such an attitude of these people is directly traceable to the lethargic mentality of many of our indolent Rajas and Maharajas who, while spending immense sums on useless and chimerical purposes, are completely deaf towards rehabilitating such useful sciences as astrology and astronomy.

What is needed is not rejection but an observational rectification of the elemnets employed by ancient astronomers.

The prefection of predictive astrology among the ancient Hindus was really marvellous, and today, we have lost that power. Even with sound mathematical basis, our predictions are generally vague and indefinite—except for a few, made by the real experts in this science. Is it because, our inductive faculty is marred by the extreme degree of precision we aim at, or are we on the wrong track? Are we not wasting much of our precious time by entering into profitless discussions and controversies as regards house division, ascribing rulership to the so-called newly discovered planets, finding the rationale of the significations of the different houses of the zodiac, etc. The greater portion of our time must be devoted to the practical study of astrology. This requires a moderate knowledge of astrological calculations. For instance, in determining Ayurdaya, Maraka Grahas (death inflicting planets) and the time of death, we should ascertain the relative sources of strength and weakness of the different planets. This requires a fair knowledge of Shadbalas. And with our present knowledge in the predictive art, we do not require to be so precise as to find out "0.000067" of an arc. We had better maintain what can be termed "minute precision" and then adopt "second precision" after we have attained proficiency in the art of predictions consistent with our present precision in calculations.

Bearing this in mind, if the reader goes through this volume, without any bias or prepossession, he will really find much useful information presented in quite an intelligible manner. Throughout the book, in the examples worked out, fractions less than half a Ghati or 30″ or of arc have been rejected. If the reader is patient enough he can consider the minutest divisions and maintain the degree of accuracy he wants.

In the determination of Madhya Lagna (10th Bhava), the Hindus do not consider the Sidereal Time of Birth. Instead, the Sun's Sayana Longitude at the birth moment and the interval between meridian-distance are taken and the Dasama Bhava Longitude determined by considering the Sidereal Time of the ascension of the Rasimanas on the equator according to the prescribed rules. Besides, the Bhogya and Bhuktha portion of a sign are found out by the application of the rule of three assuming that equal arcs ascend at equal times. These two are considered by some recent writers as fallacies or errors. But they are not fallacies at all astrologically because, perhaps the ancients thought, that it would not make much difference, whether the ascension of arc was calculated arithmetically or by more refined modern methods *for astrological purposes*. They had their own reasons, which remain inexplicable, to assume so many things, which look controvertible today. We have not the slightest justifiable ground to label them as incorrect and eulogise our own conclusions as eminently correct. We have lost the power of Yoga and we cannot see things face to face by physical aids. Hence we can neither deprecate the one nor appreciate the other. Each has its own faults and perfections and we must as far as possible adopt the Hindu method of calculations for applying Hindu astronomical principles.

BANGALORE
5th October 1935   B. V. RAMAN

DEDICATION

The Work is Respectfully Dedicated to my
revered grandfather

Bangalore Suryanarain Rao

B. V. RAMAN
The Author

SRI

CHAPTER I

The Zodiac and the Planetary System

1. Zodiac

It is a broad band or belt in the heavens extending 9 degrees on either side of the ecliptic, and known to the Hindus as Bhachakra or the Circle of Light. It is a circle and as such it knows no beginning or end. In order to measure the distance, an arbitrary point is established, which is called the first point of Aries. The zodiac revolves once in a day on its axis, from east to west.

2. The Ecliptic

The ecliptic is the Sun's path. This is known as *Apamandala* or *Ravimarga* in Sanskrit. It passes exactly through the centre of the zodiac longitudinally.

3. The Signs of the Zodiac

The ecliptic is divided into twelve equal compartments, the signs of the zodiac, each being thirty degrees in extent. Each sign has its own peculiar qualities attributed to it by the ancient Maharshis, after careful and profound observation and meditation. As already observed above, the commencement of the zodiac is reckoned from the first point of Aries. Each degree is divided into sixty minutes and each minute is further subdivided into sixty seconds, so that, the total extent of the zodiac is 21,600 minutes or 129,600 seconds.

4. Constellations

The ecliptic is marked by twenty-seven constellations or nakshatras, often called lunar mansions, because the Moon is brought into special connection with them, as traversing twenty-seven constellations and making a complete round of the ecliptic in a lunar month. Each constellation contains four padas or quarters and each quarter is equal to 3 1/3° of the celestial arc (*rekha*). In other words the whole zodiac consists of 108 padas so that each constellation measures 13° 20' of arc. The Rasis and the Nakshatras are both reckoned from the same point, *viz.*, the zero degree of longitude of Mesha (Aries), *i.e.*, the initial point of Mesha* (See Chap. II) or the first point of Aswini.

5. The Planetary System

The planetary system otherwise known as the solar system, headed by the most glorious Sun—

---
* See Varahamihira's *Brihat Jataka*—English translation by Prof. B. Suryanarain Rao.

the *Jagatchakshu*—consists of seven important planets (including the Sun himself). All the planets, save the central luminary, are held by the gravitation of the Sun and they all revolve round him, the period of revolution varying with reference to each planet. Along with these are included Rahu and Ketu—considered as *Aprakashaka grahas* or shadowy planets; moreover their importance does not seem to have been stressed upon by writers on mathematical astrology, for they are said to partake of the characteristics of the signs which they occupy, whilst writers on judicial astrology invariably recognise their influences in the analysis of a horoscope.

According to *Suryasiddhanta*, Saturn is the most distant planet from the earth; Jupiter, Mars, the Sun, Venus, Mercury and the Moon come next in the order of their distance. Uranus, Neptune and Pluto have no place in Hindu astrology.

6. Rotation and Revolution

These planetary orbs, which the ancients recognised as having powerful influences on the terrestrial phenomena, perform the double function of not only rotating on their own axes (*Bhramana*) from west to east, but also revolving round the Sun (*Bhagana*). The latter is comprehended in the astronomical nomenclature as the orbital revolution of the earth and the planets, which, for the sake of simplicity, we have preferred to call revolution.

7. Velocities of Planets

Each planet has its own rate of motion or velocity depending upon its nearness to or distance from the earth. For instance, the Moon is our nearest planet and consequently she has a very swift motion. She travels round the zodiac once in 30 lunar days; whereas, Saturn, who is the most distant from us, has the slowest motion and accordingly performs one revolution round the ecliptic in thirty years. The planets do not maintain a uniform rate of movement for various causes. The following are the approximate periods taken by each planet to make a circuit round the zodiac.

The Sun moves at the rate of roughly one degree a day or $365\frac{1}{4}$ days for one complete revolution. The Moon takes 27 days 7 hours and odd for a similar circuit. Mars takes 18 months for one revolution. Mercury requires a similar period as the Sun but his closeness to the Sun makes Mercury rather unsteady with the result that he often takes 27 days to pass through one sign. Jupiter requires roughly twelve years for a circuit. Venus has more or less the same velocity as the Sun. Saturn moves for thirty months in a sign. Rahu and Ketu take 18 months each in a sign or 18 years for a complete revolution. All the planets have Savya or direct motion, while Rahu and Ketu have *Apasavya ghati*, *i.e.*, they move from east to west.

The Velocities of Planets

		Deg.	Min.	Sec.	Para.	Paratpara	Tatpara
Sun	per day	0	59	8	10	10	24
Moon	,,	13	10	34	52	3	49
Mars	,,	0	31	26	28	11	9
Mercury	,,	4	5	32	20	41	51
Jupiter	,,	0	4	59	8	48	35
Venus	,,	1	36	7	43	37	15
Saturn	,,	0	2	0	22	53	25

60 Tatparas = 1 Paratpara
60 Paratparas = 1 para
60 Paras = 1 Second

The above information is culled out from an ancient astronomical work and the reader is referred to works on modern astronomy for fuller and more detailed information.

8. Retrogression and Acceleration

When the distance of any one planet from the Sun exceeds a particular limit, it becomes retrograde, *i.e.*, when the planet goes from perihelion (the part of a planet's orbit nearest to the Sun) to aphelion (the part of a planet's orbit most distant from the Sun) as it recedes from the Sun, it gradually loses the power of the Sun's gravitation and consequently, to gain it, it retrogrades; and when the planet comes from aphelion to perihelion, nearer and nearer to the Sun the gravitation of the Sun grows more and more powerful, so that the velocity of the planet is accelerated, *i.e.*, the state of *Athichara* is entered into. All the planets are subject to retrogression and acceleration excepting the Sun and the Moon, let alone the *Aprakashaka grahas*. Hence we find that there is no uniformity in the velocities of planets, that they vary at different parts of the orbits and that the planetary orbits are elliptical. The vakra, athichara, etc., are caused, according to *Suryasiddhanta*, by the invisible forces *Seeghrochcha*, *Mandochcha* and *Patha*. The phenomenon of retrogression has been elaborately discussed in my *Graha and Bhava Balas*.

The importance of *vakra*, etc., of planets, so far as it is necessary for astrological purposes, will be dealt with in its proper place. Those who wish to soar into the higher regions of astronomy will do well to study such celebrated works as *Suryasiddhanta*, *Panchasiddhantika*, etc., of illustrious authors of yore, in whose luminous expositions of this celestial science, the inquiring mind is sure to find much more than what is sought for.

CHAPTER II

Preliminaries Explained

9. Rasis and Their Extent

No.	Sign	Its English Equivalent	Its Symbol	Its Extent	
1.	Mesha	Aries	♈	0°	30°
2.	Vrishabha	Taurus	♉	30	60
3.	Mithuna	Gemini	♊	60	90
4.	Kataka	Cancer	♋	90	120
5.	Simha	Leo	♌	120	150
6.	Kanya	Virgo	♍	150	180
7.	Thula	Libra	♎	180	210
8.	Vrischika	Scorpio	♏	210	240
9.	Dhanus	Sagittarius	♐	240	270
10.	Makara	Capricorn	♑	270	300
11.	Kumbha	Aquarius	♒	300	330
12.	Meena	Pisces	♓	330	360

10. Nakshatras and Their Extent

No.	Rasi (Sign)	Nakshatra (Constellation)	Pada (Quarter)	Space on the ecliptic from 0° Aries	
1.	Aries	1. Aswini	4	13°	20
		2. Bharani	4	26	40
		3. Krittika	1	30	00
2.	Taurus	Krittika	3	40	0
		4. Rohini	4	53	20
		5. Mrigasira	2	60	0
3.	Gemini	Mrigasira	2	66	40
		6. Aridra	4	80	0
		7. Punarvasu	3	90	0

No.	Rasi (Sign)	Nakshatra (Constellation)	Pada (Quarter)	Space on the ecliptic from 0° Aries	
4.	Cancer	Punarvasu	1	93	20
		8. Pushyami	4	106	40
		9. Aslesha	4	120	0
5.	Leo	10. Makha	4	133	20
		11. Pubba	4	146	40
		12. Uttara	1	150	0
6.	Virgo	Uttara	3	160	0
		13. Hasta	4	173	20
		14. Chitta	2	180	0
7.	Libra	Chitta	2	186	40
		15. Swati	4	200	0
		16. Visakha	3	210	0
8.	Scorpio	Visakha	1	213	20
		17. Anuradha	4	226	40
		18. Jyeshta	4	240	0
9.	Sagittarius	19. Moola	4	253	20
		20. Poorvashadha	4	266	40
		21. Uttarashadha	1	270	0
10.	Capricorn	Uttarashadha	3	280	0
		22. Sravana	4	293	30
		23. Dhanishta	2	300	0
11.	Aquarius	Dhanishta	2	306	40
		24. Satabhisha	4	320	0
		25. Poorvabhadra	3	330	0
12.	Pisces	Poorvabhadra	1	333	20
		26. Uttarabhadra	4	346	40
		27. Revati	4	360	0

The above table may be interpreted thus. It will be seen that there are 27 constellations comprising the 12 signs. For instance, take Aries. You will find that 4 quarters of Aswini (13° 20′), 4 of Bharani (13° 20′) and 1 of Krittika (3° 20′)—on the whole 9 quarters—constitute it. Again, the remaining 3 of Krittika (10°), the 4 of Rohini (13° 20′) and 2 of Mrigasira (6° 40′) make up Taurus and so on. Of what use this table will be, the reader will realise after he has gone through some more pages. For the present, suffice it to say that he must be quite familiar with it in order to understand the information set forth in subsequent chapters.

Note.—In the characteristics of the signs and planets which I am giving below, such information as has a direct bearing upon and is involved in the mathematical calculations, has been included. All other details necessary for predictions, which can be gathered from any astrological work, have been scrupulously omitted.

11. **Movable Signs**
    Aries, Cancer, Libra and Capricorn.

12. **Fixed Signs**
    Taurus, Leo, Scorpio and Aquarius.

13. **Common Signs**
    Gemini, Virgo, Sagittarius and Pisces.

14. **Odd Signs**
    Aries, Gemini, Leo, Libra, Sagittarius and Aquarius.

15. Even Signs

Taurus, Cancer, Virgo, Scorpio, Capricorn and Pisces.

16. Signs of Long Ascension

Cancer, Leo, Virgo, Libra, Scorpio and Sagittarius.

17. Signs of Short Ascension

Capricorn, Aquarius, Pisces, Aries, Taurus and Gemini.

This order has to be reversed for places south of the equator in Articles 16 and 17.

18. Sirodaya Signs (Rising by head)

Gemini, Leo, Virgo, Libra, Scorpio and Aquarius.

19. Prustodaya Signs (Rising by hinder part)

Aries, Taurus, Cancer, Sagittarius and Capricorn.

The Sirodaya signs excepting Gemini are powerful during the day. The Prustodaya signs including Gemini are powerful during the night. The former are also called Nocturnal signs and the latter the Diurnal signs. Pisces and Gemini form a combination of the two and are called Ubhayodaya Rasis.

20. Quadrants (Kendras)

1, 4, 7 and 10.

21. Trines (Trikonas)
1, 5 and 9.

22. Succeedent Houses (Panaparas)
2, 5, 8 and 11.

23. Cadent Houses (Apoklimas)
3, 6, 9 and 12 (9th being a trikona must be omitted).

24. Oopachayas
3, 6, 10 and 11.

25. Planetary Ownerships
Aries and Scorpio are ruled by Mars; Taurus and Libra by Venus; Gemini and Virgo by Mercury; Cancer by the Moon; Leo by the Sun; Sagittarius and Pisces by Jupiter; and Capricorn and Aquarius by Saturn.

26. Exaltation
The Sun has his deep exaltation in the 10th degree of Aries; Moon 3rd of Taurus; Mars 28th of Capricorn; Mercury 15th of Virgo; Jupiter 5th of Cancer; Venus 27th of Pisces; and Saturn 20th of Libra.

27. Debilitation
The 7th house or the 180th degree from the place of exaltation is the place of debilitation or fall. The Sun is debilitated in the 10th degree of Libra, the Moon in the 3rd of Scorpio and so on.

28. Good and Evil Planets

Jupiter, Venus, full Moon and well-associated Mercury are good or benefic planets and new Moon, badly associated Mercury, the Sun, Saturn and Mars are evil or malefic planets. From the 8th day of the bright half of the lunar month the Moon is full or benefic. He is weak from the 8th day of the dark half.

29. Sexes

Jupiter, Mars and the Sun are males; Venus and the Moon are females; and Mercury and Saturn are eunuchs.

30. Moola Trikonas

Sun's Moola Trikona is Leo (0°-20°); Moon—Taurus (4°-20°); Mercury—Virgo (16°-20); Jupiter—Sagittarius (0°-10); Mars—Aries (0°-12°); Venus—Libra (0°-15°) and Saturn—Aquarius (0°-20°).

31. Planetary Relations

By friendship we mean that the rays of the one planet are intensified by those of the other, declared as his friend, while the same rays will be counteracted by a planet who is an enemy.

Friendship can be both permanent (*Naisargika*) and temporary (*Tatkalika*). (See my *Graha and Bhava Balas* for Tatkalika friendship.)

Permanent Relationship

Planets (Grahas)	Friends (Mitras)	Neutrals (Samas)	Enemies (Satrus)
Sun	Moon, Mars, Jupiter.	Mercury.	Saturn, Venus.
Moon	Sun, Mercury.	Mars, Jupiter, Venus, Saturn.	None.
Mars	Sun, Moon, Jupiter.	Venus, Saturn.	Mercury.
Mercury	Sun, Venus.	Mars, Jupiter, Saturn.	Moon.
Jupiter	Sun, Moon, Mars.	Saturn.	Mercury, Venus.
Venus	Mercury, Saturn.	Mars, Jupiter.	Sun, Moon.
Saturn	Mercury, Venus.	Jupiter.	Sun, Moon, Mars.

The practical applicability of some of these characteristics of planets and signs have been explained in my *Graha and Bhava Balcs*, etc.

32. Karakas

Each planet is supposed to be the karaka of certain events in life. Many function as producing, rather promoting the incidents ascribed to them.

Name	English equivalent	Symbol	Karaka of	Indicator of
Surya	Sun	☉	Pitru	Father
Chandra	Moon	☽	Matru	Mother
Angaraka	Mars	♂	Bhratru	Brother
Budha	Mercury	☿	Karma	Profession
Guru	Jupiter	♃	Putra	Children
Sukra	Venus	♀	Kalatra	Wife or Husband
Sani	Saturn	♄	Ayus	Longevity
Rahu	Dragon's Head	☊	Mathamaha	Material relations
Ketu	Dragon's Tail	☋	Pithamaha	Paternal relations

33. Bhavas

These correspond roughly to the 'Houses' of Western astrology. The most powerful point in a Bhava is its Madhya Bhaga or mid-point whereas he first point is the most powerful in a 'Western House'. There are twelve Bhavas and each controls, rather, signifies certain important events and incidents.

Bhava	House	Signification
(1) Thanubhava	First House	build, body, appearance.
(2) Dhanabhava	Second House	family, source of death, property, vision.
(3) Bhratrubhava	Third House	intelligence, brothers, sisters.
(4) Sukhabhava	Fourth House	vehicles, general happiness, education, mother.

	Bhava	*House*	*Signification*
(5)	Putrabhava	Fifth House	fame, children.
(6)	Satrubhava	Sixth House	debts, diseases, misery, enemies.
(7)	Kalatrabhava	Seventh House	wife or husband, death.
(8)	Ayurbhava	Eighth House	longevity, gifts.
(9)	Dharmabhava	Ninth House	god, guru, father, travels, piety.
(10)	Karmabhava	Tenth House	occupation, karma, philosophical knowledge.
(11)	Labhabhava	Eleventh House	gains.
(12)	Vrayabhava	Twelfth House	loss, moksha.

34. The Astrological Measure

The various sources of strength and weakness of the planets and Bhavas are estimated by certain units or measures. They are Rupas, Virupas and Prarupas. 60 Prarupas are equal to 1 Virupa and 60 Virupas make 1 Rupa.

Astronomical Terminology

35. The Axis and Poles of the Earth

The axis of the earth is that diameter about which it revolves from west to east with a uniform motion. The poles of the earth are its points where its axis meets its surface and they are the north pole and the south pole.

36. The Earth's Equator (Vishvarekha)

This is an imaginary line running round the earth half-way between the two poles. The equator divides the earth into a northern and a southern hemisphere.

37. The Latitude (Akshamsa)

The latitude of a place is its distance north or south of the equator, measured as an angle, on its own terrestrial meridian. It is reckoned in degrees, minutes and seconds from 0° to 90°, northwards or southwards according as the place lies in the northern or the southern hemisphere.

38. The Longitude (Rekhamsa)

The longitude of the place is its distance east or west of the meridian or Greenwich (Ujjain according to the Hindus) measured as an angle. It is expressed in degrees, minutes and seconds, east or west of Greenwich according to where the place lies. It is also reckoned in time at the rate of 24 hours for 360° or 4 minutes for every degree.

39. The Celestial Equator (Nadivritta)

This is a great circle of the celestial sphere marked out by the indefinite extension of the plane of the terrestrial equator.

40. The Celestial Latitude (Kshepa)

This is the angular distance of a heavenly body from the ecliptic.

41. The Declination (Kranti)

This is the angular distance of a heavenly body from the celestial equator. It is positive or negative according as the celestial object is situated in the northern or the southern hemisphere.

CHAPTER III

The Ayanamsa

42. Equinoctial Points

The celestial equator and the ecliptic intersect each other at two points; because, twice a year the Sun crosses the equator. On these two days the duration of day and night will be equal all the world over. These two points are known as the equinoctial points, or the Vernal Equinox and the Autumnal Equinox.

43. Precession of the Equinoxes

It has been observed and proved mathematically that each year at the time when the Sun reaches his equinoctial point of Aries 0, when throughout the earth, the day and night are equal in length, the position of the earth in reference to some fixed star is nearly $50\frac{1}{3}''$ of space farther west than the earth was, at the same equinoctial movement of the previous year. It is not merely the earth or the solar system, but the entire zodiac that is subjected to this westward motion. This slight increment—retrograde motion of the equinoxes—is known as the Precession of the Equinoxes.

44. Movable and Fixed Zodiacs

We have seen from the above that the vernal equinox slips backwards from its original position —recognised as the star Revati—by the Hindus. The zodiac which reckons the first degree of Aries from the equinoctial point which has a precession every year is the movable zodiac, whilst, in the case of the fixed zodiac, the first degree of Aries begins from a particular star in the Revati group of stars which is fixed. The movable zodiac is also termed as the zodiac of signs which the fixed zodiac is known as the Zodiac of Constellations, as its signs are almost identical with the constellations bearing the same names.

45. The Sayana and the Nirayana Systems

The system of astronomy which recognises the movable zodiac belongs to the Sayana school while that which considers the fixed zodiac is termed as the Nirayana System. The Sayana is the one employed by Western astrologers for predictive purposes while the Hindu astrologers use the fixed zodiac. Of late there is a movement in the Western astrological circles in favour of the Nirayana zodiac and many leading astrologers have shown their preference for what they call the sidereal zodiac, another name for the Nirayana system.

46. The Ayanamsa

The distance between the Hindu first point and

the Vernal Equinox, measured at an epoch, is known as the Ayanamsa.

47. Varahamihira's Observations

Even Varahamihira, one of the most celebrated of ancient writers in India, perpetuates and carries on the teachings of his far more ancient predecessors in marking the distinction between the two zodiacs and referring all the astrological observations to the fixed zodiac. He states, that in his time, the summer solstice coincided with the first degree of Cancer, and the winter solstice with the first degree of Capricorn, whereas at one time the summer solstice coincided with the middle of the Aslesha.

48. Exact Date of Coincidence not known

The exact period when both the zodiacs coincided in the first point is not definitely known and accordingly the Ayanamsa—the precessional distance—varies from 19° to 23°. The star which marked the first point seems to have somehow disappeared though some believe that it is 11 east of the star Pisces. A number of dates are given as the year of the coincidence, *viz.*, 361 A.D., 394 A.D., 397 A.D., 498 A.D., 559 A.D., etc.; which to accept, and which to reject, has been a matter of considerable doubt. No definite proof is available in favour of any one of the dates given above. No amount of mere speculation would be of any use especially in such matters. Some attribute these differences to the supposed errors in Hindu observations. Whatever they may be it is not our purpose here to enter into any sort of discussion which would be purely of academical interest and absolutely outside our limits. As such without worrying the reader with the technicalities involved in the discussion of the most vital question of the Precession of the Equinoxes we shall directly enter into setting below a simple method for ascertaining the Ayanamsa, which will serve the purpose of any scientific astrologer and which would enable the reader to thoroughly understand and follow the principles described in the following pages.

49. Use of Ayanamsa

The Indian adepts in the celestial science realising that the degrees of the fixed zodiac have a permanent relation with the star-points, and that the movable zodiac does not give us a definite position both for observation and experiment and to arrive at logical conclusions, have been advocating the Nirayana positions of planets for all predictive purposes. These should be arrived at after the necessary calculations are made according to Sayana and then the Ayanamsa subtracted from such positions. For astrological purposes, it would be quite sufficient, if we know how to determine the Ayanamsa for any particular year. Since the object of this book is not to enter into any discusion about the superiority of this or that system, or the justification of adopting any particular value as the Ayanamsa, but to clearly describe and expound principles necessary for correct computation of a horoscope mathematically according to the prescribed rules and to determine the various sources of strength and weakness of planets and discover other details that are within the reach of mathematical astrology and thus clear the way for making correct predictions, we do not propose to lay any further stress on this question of Ayanamsa.

The Longitudes of the Houses (Bhava Sphutas), Rasimanas (Oblique Ascensions) and other important calculations are all computed for Sayana Rasis. From these the Ayanamsa is subtracted and the Nirayana Bhavas, etc., are obtained. In other words, every one of the Hindu astrological calculations, which is at first based upon the Sayana Rasis, is eventually subjected to Nirayana reduction. All these indicate the absolute necessity for Ayanamsa.

). Determination of (Approximate) Ayanamsa

(1) Substract 397 from the year of birth (A.D.).
(2) Multiply the remainder by $50\frac{1}{3}''$ and reduce the product into degrees, minutes and seconds.

Example 1. *Determine the Ayanamsa for 1912 A.D.*
$1912 - 397 = 1515 \times 50\ 1/3'' = 76,255''$
$76,255'' = 21° 10' 55''$.

Example 2. *Find the Ayanamsa for 1918 A.D.*
$1918 - 397 = 1521 \times 50\ 1/3'' = 76,557'' = 21° 15' 57''$.

The slipping back of the movable zodiac in a year is so small that for odd days, we can conveniently ignore it. But the Ayanamsa for the moment can be determined by considering the precession for the odd days also.

CHAPTER IV

Rasimanas

51. Geographic and Geocentric Latitudes

The latitudes of places marked in any ordinary atlas are geographical latitudes. Because they are calculated on the supposition that the earth is a perfect sphere, while on the other hand the flattened ends at the two poles make it a spheroid the latitude, measured from the true centre of the spheroid, is the actual or geocentric latitude. For astrological purposes, it would be hardly worthwhile making any distinction whatever between the geocentric and geographic latitude. For instance the geographic latitude of Bangalore is 12° 57′ and its geocentric 12° 52′. We can adopt the former alone for astrological calculations.

52. Rasimanas

Rasimanas mean the rising periods of the twelve signs of the zodiac. According to the Hindus it is not possible to find out the actual Lagna (Ascendant) in a horoscope or the different Bhavas (Houses) or the sunrise and sunset in any place without a knowledge of the Rasimanas, which vary from Akshamsa (latitude) to Akshamsa. It must be noted that the Rasimana is always given in Sayana (with precession), that is to say, the time of oblique ascension is computed for the signs of the movable zodiac. From this is subtracted the Ayanamsa and the appropriate time of the oblique ascension and the result is the Nirayana Rasimana. If the division of the zodiac into 12 signs be taken to commence from the equinoctial point, their rising periods for any particular place will not vary from year to year.

53. Charakhandas

The duration of the signs of zodiac varies in the different degrees of latitude which can be ascertained by the Charakhandas (ascensional differences) of the particular latitude. Say, for instance, two men are born at the same time, one in Bangalore and the other in Berlin. Their latitudes are different. The rising periods of the signs in Bangalore must be quite different from those in Berlin. The sunrise and sunset in both places cannot be the same. Therefore the rising periods in the different latitudes must be definitely known before casting a horoscope.

These Charakhandas (ascensional differences) referred to above, in Indian sidereal time, the unit of which is an Asu (which is the equivalent of four seconds in English sidereal time) are, in accordance with certain definite rules, added to or subtracted from, the time of the Right Ascension (Dhruva) of the various Sayana Rasis, in order to get their

Oblique Ascension (Chara). Since the Chara (period of oblique ascension) and the Dhruva (period of right ascension) are identically the same for the Vishavarekha (equator) the ascensional difference is zero (shunya) for all the places situated on the equator. The ascensional difference is the same, in respect of the same sign, for places situated in the same latitude.

To be more clear, the rising periods on the equator where the Charakhanda is zero-being known, it is possible to calculate the Rasimanas for any latitude, provided its Charakhandas are also known.

54. Rising Periods on the Equator

The rising periods of the zodiacal signs reckoned from Sayana Mesha are thus distributed on the equator (0° Latitude).

ASUS

Aries	Virgo	1674	Libra	Pisces
Taurus	Leo	1795	Scorpio	Aquarius
Gemini	Cancer	1931	Sagittarius	Capricorn

(6 Asus = 1 Vighatika = 24 Seconds.
60 Vighatikas = 1 Ghatika = 24 Minutes)

The above means that it takes Aries, Virgo, Libra and Pisces 1674 Asus or 4 Gh. 39 Vig. (or $1^h\ 51^m\ 36^s$) to rise at the eastern horizon on the equator and so on.

55. Determination of Rasimanas

From or to the rising periods on the equator, the Charakhandas (ascensional differences) of the required place from Aries to Gemini and from Capricorn to Pisces are subtractive* and from Cancer to Virgo and from Libra to Sagittarius are additive. That is, in the case of from Aries to Gemini and from Capricorn to Pisces, subtract the Charakhandas and from Cancer to Virgo and from Libra to Sagittarius add the Charakhandas of the required place, and the rising periods of signs there are obtained. These must be applied to any one of four triads as given above, into which the zodiacal signs are divided—commencing always from the Sayana Mesha, *i.e.*, the first 30 from the equinoctial point.

---
* In North Latitudes.

Determination of Rasimanas

The following examples will clear the meaning:—

Example 3.—*Find the Rasimanas at 13° N. Lat. whose Charakhandas are 162, 130 and 53 Asus respectively.*

Signs	Rising periods at 0° Lat. (in Asus)		Charakhandas on 13° N. Latitude	Times of oblique ascension at 13° N. Latitude (in Asus)	Times of oblique ascension at 13° N. Latitude (in Ghatis)	
					*Gh.	Vig.
1. Aries	1,674	—	162	1,512	4	12
2. Taurus	1,795	—	130	1,695	4	37
3. Gemini	1,931	—	53	1,878	5	13
4. Cancer	1,931	+	53	1,984	5	31
5. Leo	1,795	+	130	1,925	5	21
6. Virgo	1,674	+	162	1,836	5	6
7. Libra	1,674	+	162	1,836	5	6
8. Scorpio	1,795	+	130	1,925	5	21
9. Sagittarius	1,931	+	53	1,984	5	31
10. Capricorn	1,931	—	53	1,878	5	13
11. Aquarius	1,795	—	130	1,665	4	37
12. Pisces	1,674	—	162	1,512	4	12
	21,600			21,600	60	0

---

* Fractions have been rounded off : *e.g. G. 5-20 5/6 = G. 5-21*

A Manual of Hindu Astrology

Example 4.—*Find Rasimanas on 5° 32'* * *N. Lat. whose Charakhandas are 921, 737 and 307 respectively.*

Signs	Rising periods at 0° Lat. (in Asus)	Chara- khandas at 51° 32' N. Lat.	Times of oblique ascension at 51° 32' N. Lat. (in Asus)	Times of oblique ascension 51° 32' N. Lat. (in Ghatis) Gh. Vig.
1. Aries	1,674	— 921	753	2 5
2. Taurus	1,795	— 737	1,058	2 57
3. Gemini	1,931	— 307	1,624	4 31
4. Cancer	1,931	+ 307	2,238	6 13
5. Leo	1,795	+ 737	2,532	7 2
6. Virgo	1,674	+ 921	2,595	7 12
7. Libra	1,674	+ 921	2,595	7 12
8. Scorpio	1,795	+ 737	2,532	7 2
9. Sagittarius	1,931	+ 307	2,238	6 13
10. Capricorn	1,931	— 307	1,624	4 31
11. Aquarius	1,795	— 737	1,058	2 57
12. Pisces	1,674	— 921	753	2 5
	21,600		21,600	60 0

(See Table 1 for Charakhanda for latitudes 1°60)

---

* The Charakhandas for 52° are considered.

Determination of Rasimanas 61

56. Duration of Signs in South Latitudes

The additive and subtractive Charakhandas of North Latitude become subtractive and additive, respectively, in case of South Latitudes. For example *add* 162 to 1674 instead of subtracting, and the duration of Aries on 13° S. Latitude is obtained. It is to be noted that signs of short ascension in N. Latitudes are signs of long ascension in S. Latitudes.

Example 5.— *Find the Rasimanas at 37° 50' South Latitude, whose Charakhandas are 562, 450 and 187 respectively.*

	Signs	Rising period at 0° Lat. (in Asus)	Chara- khandas at 37° 57' S. Lat.	Times of oblique ascension at 37° 57' S. Lat. (in Asus)	Times of oblique ascension at 37° 57' S. Lat. (in Ghatis)
					Gh. Vig.
1.	Aries	1,674	+ 562	2,236	6 13
2.	Taurus	1,795	+ 450	2,245	6 14
3.	Gemini	1,931	+ 187	2,118	5 53
4.	Cancer	1,931	— 187	1,744	4 50
5.	Leo	1,795	— 450	1,345	3 44
6.	Virgo	1,674	— 562	1,112	3 5
7.	Libra	1,674	— 562	1,112	3 5
8.	Scorpio	1,795	— 450	1,345	3 44
9.	Sagittarius	1,931	— 187	1,744	4 50
10.	Capricorn	1,931	+ 187	2,118	5 53
11.	Aquarius	1,795	+ 450	2,245	6 14
12.	Pisces	1,674	+ 562	2,236	6 13
		21,600		21,600	60 0

CHAPTER V
Sunrise and Sunset

57. Apparent Time of Rising and Setting of the Sun

The exact moment when the Sun first appears at the eastern horizon of a place is time of sunrise there. Since the Sun has a definite diameter, the interval between the moment of the appearance of the first ray at the horizon and the moment at which the Sun is just clear off the horizon, is some 5 or 6 minutes. If this is so, which represents the exact moment of sunrise ? It has been acknowledged that it is the moment at which the centre of the solar disc rises at the eastern horizon that marks the sunrise at the particular place. It must also be noted that on account of the refraction of the solar rays due to the various strata enveloping the earth, the Sun is not really below the horizon when he appears to be so but is really below the horizon by about a few minutes of arc (Rekha). But we can take the apparent time as almost correct and need not worry ourselves with the so-called delicate correct time of rising.

58. Apparent Noon

This is marked when the centre of the Sun is exactly on the meridian of the place. The apparent noon is almost the same for all places.

59. Ahas and Ratri

Ahas is the duration of the day, *i.e.*, the duration of time, from sunrise to sunset, and Ratri is the duration of time, from sunset to sunrise. On the equator, the Ahas and Ratri are always 30 ghatis or 12 hours each, while in other latitudes, the sum of Ahas and Ratri will be 24 hours, whereas the interval between sunrise and sunset and *vice versa* varies, this variation depending upon the declination of the Sun and the latitude of the place.

The duration of *Ratri* in a place expressed in arc corresponds to the Sun's nocturnal arc and that of the day to his diurnal arc. If we know either of these arcs, we can find out sunrise and sunset.

In dealing with the question of the Procession of the Equinoxes, we have called attention to the fact that on the days when the Sun occupies the equinoctical points, *i.e.*, twice a year, he is visible for 12 hours at all places and invisible for a similar period. On these two days the declination (kranti) of the Sun is zero.

During his northerly course, when he has a north declination, the duration of days is longer than that of nights, *i.e.*, he is visible for a longer period in north latitudes, while the reverse holds good for south latitudes. During his southerly course, when he has a south declination, the duration of days is longer than that of nights in south latitudes, and the reverse holds good for north latitudes.

60. Hindu Method of Determination of Sunrise and of Sunset

First of all note the latitude of the place for which sunrise and sunset are to be determined and then its Charakhandas. Find out the position of Nirayana Sun* at approximate sunrise on that day. This can be done from any local reliable almanac. (See Chapter VII for determining longitudes of planets.)

To this add Ayanamsa and the Sayana Sun at sunrise is obtained: or the position of the Sayana Sun can be obtained by means of any modern ephemeris in which the position of planets are to be found for Greenwich mean noon. By converting the approximate time (local) of sunrise to Greenwich mean time, the position of Sayana Sun—for sunrise can be found out. (See Chapter VI for Conversion of Time.) Then find out the Bhuja (distance from the nearest equinoctical point) as follows:

If the Sayana longitude of the Sun be less than 90° (*i.e.*, the first three signs) it itself represents the Sun's Bhuja ; if it is more than 90° and less than 180°, subtract it from 180° and the result is Bhuja ; if it is more than 180° and less than 270° (*i.e.*, more than 6 signs and less than 9 signs) *subtract* 180° from the Sun's Sayana longitude, the result represents Bhuja ;

---
* The solar date marked in Hindu almanacs may be roughly taken as representing Sun's Nirayana longitude at sunrise on the particular day.

Determination of Sunrise

and if the Sayana longitude of the Sun is more than 270° and less than 360° (more than 9 signs and less than 12 signs) subtract it from 360° and the result is Bhuja of the Sun.

If the Sun's Sayana
longitude is—   Bhuja is
(1) between   0°   90°   Sun's Sayana long. itself.
(2) ,,   90   180   180°−Sun's Sayana long.
(3) ,,   180   270   Sun's Sayana long.−180°.
(4) ,,   270   360   360°−Sun's Sayana long.

The Charakhandas (ascensional differences) given in three numbers are called the Adi (first), Madhya (middle) and Anthya (last) Charakhandas. The Adicharakhanda itself will be the first khanda; this *plus* the madhya, the second khanda; and the sum of the three (Charakhandas), the third khanda.

Now divide the Bhuja (if it is more than 30°) by 30. The quotient represents the khanda. Keep the remainder as it is and then apply the rule:

As 30 degrees : the remainder : : the Charakhanda (Madhya, if Bhuja is more than 30° and less than 60° and Anthya if it is more than 60° and less than 90°): the required quantity.

This required quantity must be added to the equivalent of the khandas represented by the quotient obtained by dividing the Bhuja by 30. The result is *chara*.

If the Bhuja is less than 30° then apply the rule:

As 30 degrees : the degree (represented by Bhuja : : the Adicharakhanda : the required quantity.

Then the quantity itself will be chara.

If the Sayana Sun is in Uttara (north) Gola (hemisphere), *i.e.*, from Aries to Virgo, add chara to 15 ghatis (6 hours). If he is in the southern Gola (from Libra to Pisces) subtract this from 15 ghatis. The result is Dinardha (half diurnal duration). Twice this is the length of day. This deducted from 60 ghatis (24 hours) gives the length of night. Convert Dinardha into hours, etc., and add and subtract this figure to and from 12 noon respectively. The apparent time of sunset and of sunrise respectively of the place are obtained.

Example 6.—*Find the length of day of night and the apparent time of sunrise and of sunset at a place on 13° N. Lat. and 5h. 10m. 20s. E. Long. on 16th October 1918 (A.D.)*,

	Adi (First)	Madhya (Middle)	Anthya (Last)
Charakhandas —	162	130 and	53 (in Asus)
		or	
	27	21.7 and	8.8 (in Vighatis)
	(27)	(22)	(9)
	I	II	III
∴ Khandas =	27	49 and	58

Nirayana Sun at approximate
sunrise (6 a.m.)   =   ...   180°   55'   0"
Ayanamsa   =   ...   21   15   57
∴ Sayana Sun   =   ...   202°   10' 57"
= 202° 11' = Libra 22° 11'

Since the Sayana Longitude of the Sun is between
180°—270° apply Rule 3 to find out the Bhuja.

Rule 3.—Sun's Sayana Long.—180° = Bhuja.
202° 11' − 180° = 22° 11'.

Since in the above, Bhuja, viz., 22° 11' is less than 30°, apply the following rule to get Chara :

As 30 degrees : the degrees represented by Bhuja : :
    Adicharakhanda : the required quantity $=x$.

$\therefore$ 30 : 22° 11' : : 27 : the required quantity $=x$.

$\therefore x = \dfrac{22° 11'}{30} \times 27 = 19.96$ vighatis or 20 vig.

$\therefore x = 20$ vighatis = Chara itself.

$\therefore$ Sayana Sun is in Dakshina Gola (between Libra and Pisces)

$\therefore$ Dinardha   = Gh. (15.0) — Gh. (0.20)
  (Half diurnal duration)   = Gh. 14.40.

$\therefore$ Length of day = Gh. 14–40 × 2 = Gh. 29–20.

$\therefore$ Length of night = Gh. 60 — Gh. (29–20) = Gh. 30–40.

   Dinardha = Gh. 14–40 ; in hours = 5h. 52m.

   12 noon — 5h. 52m. = 6h. 8m.

$\therefore$ **Apparent Time of Sunrise** = 6h. 8m. (A.M.)

12 noon + 5h. 52m. = 5h. 52m. (P.M.) sunset.

Example 7.—*Find the length of day and of night and apparent time of sunset and of sunrise at 36° N. Lat. on 7th January 1932.*

Charakhandas	=	522.6,	418.08 and	174.18 (in Asus)
	=	87	70	and 29 (in Vighatis)
		I	II	III
= Khandas	=	87	157	186

		S.	D.	M.	S.
Niryana Sun	=	8	24	2	13
Ayanamsa	=	+0	21	27	41
$\therefore$ Sayana Sun	=	9	15	29	54

                           = 15° 30' Capricorn.

	S.	D.	M.
	12	0	0
—Sayana Sun =	9	15	30
Bhuja =	2	14	30 = 74° 30′

Divide Bhuja by $30 = \dfrac{74° \ 30'}{30} =$ Khanda 2 and remainder 14° 30′

As $30 : 14\tfrac{1}{2}° : : 29 :$ the required quantity $= x$.

$$= x = \dfrac{14\tfrac{1}{2}}{30} \times 29 = 14 \text{ Vighatis.}$$

14 Vig. + 157 (Khanda II) = 171 Vig. = Chara.

Gh. 15 − (2–51 Gh.) = 12–9 Gh. = Dinardha 4h. 51m. 36s.

∴ Gh. 24–18 = length of day.

∴ Gh. 35–42 = length of night.

12 noon − 4h. 51m. 36s. = 7h. 8m. 24s. (A.M.)
sunrise (Apparent time) = 7h. 8m. 24s. (A.M.)

12 noon + 4h. 51m. 36s. = 4h. 51m. 36s. (P.M.)
sunset (Apparent time)

I have given above the Hindu method of finding out the apparent time of sunrise and of sunset. Some say, that this method is riddled with certain errors. I have spoken sufficiently about the supposed errors that have crept into Hindu calculations in the Introduction to this book. I shall also give below the modern method of the calculation of sunrise and sunset and the reader can adopt whichever he prefers. I shall apply this method to the example worked out for the Hindu method so that the results in both the cases may be compared. Those who want to adopt the Hindu method may do so ; and

Charakhandas

those who are in a position to work out problems in trigonometry may employ the modern method. I have also given in the Appendix, Tables of sunrise and sunset for every 5 days for intervals of 10° of latitude. By interpolation sunrise and sunset for the required date and degree can be obtained.

61. Modern Method of Determination of Apparent Time of Sunrise and of Sunset*

First convert the local approximate time of sunset (or sunrise) into Greenwich Mean Time (see next chapter) for which ascertain Sun's declination from the ephemeris. Note down the latitude of the place and apply the following formula :

Log Tan. Dec. of Sun + Log Tan. Lat. of place = Log Sin Ascensional Difference.

Subtract ascensional difference from 90° if Dec. is South and add Asc. difference to 90° if Dec. is North.

(The reverse holds good for places in south latitudes)

Convert the resulting degree into hours, minutes, etc., at 15° = 1 hour. The result is local apparent time of setting. This subtracted from 12 hours gives local apparent time of sunrise.

Example 8.—*Find the apparent time of sunrise and of sunset at a place on 13° N. Lat. and 5h. 10m. 20s. E. Long. on 16th October 1918.*

Approximate time of sunset = 6 p.m.
This converted to G.M.T. H. M. S.
(Greenwich Mean Time) = 12 49 40 (P.M.).

---

* There is a slight difference between the results obtained according to Hindu and modern methods which may be safely ignored *for astrological purposes.*

The difference between Greenwich Mean Noon and G.M.T. is only 49m. 40s. Therefore we may take the declination of the Sun at G.M.N. on 16th October. The declination may be determined for 12h. 49m. 40s. or 12–50 p.m. by considering Sun's motion (in dec.) in 24 hrs. and thus his proportional motion for 50m.

Decn. of the Sun on October 16th at G.M.N. = 8° 41′ S.

∴ Log Tan 8° 41′ + Log Tan 13° = Log. Sin Asc. Diff*

= 9.1839 + 9.3634 = 18.5473 = Sin 2° (roughly)

∴ Log Sin Asc. Difference = Log Sin 2°

∴ Asc. Difference = 2°

∴ Declination is south : subtract this from 90°

∴ 90° − 2° = 88°

88° 0′ − 5h. (P.M.) = Local apparent time of setting.

∴ 12h. − 5h. 52m. = 6h. 8m. (A.M.) = Local apparent time of rising.

Example 9.—*Find the apparent time of sunrise and of sunset on 7th January 1932 at a place whose Lat. is 36° N. and Long. 90° E.*

Approximate time of sunset = 6 p.m.

This converted into G.M.T. = 12 noon.

Since G.M.T. corresponding to 6 p.m. has become the same as Greenwich Mean Noon, we may take the declination of the Sun at G.M.T. on 7th January.

∴ Sun's declination at 12 noon (G.M.T.) or at the sunset at the required place = 22° 30′ S.

∴ Log Tan 22° 30′ + Log Tan 36° = Log Sin Asc. Diff.

= 9.6172 + 9.8613 = 19.4785 = 9.4785 = Log. Sin 17° 31′

∴ Log Sin Asc. Difference = Log Sin 17° 31′

∴ Asc. Difference = 17° 31′

---

* Seven figure logarithmic Tables may be consulted for greater accuracy.

Equation of Time

∴ Dec. is South subtract this from 90°

∴ 90° − 17° 31′ = 72° 29′

72° 29′ = 4h. 49m. 56s. = Local apparent time of setting = 4h. 49m. 56s. (P.M.)

∴ 12h. − 4h. 49m. 56s. = 7h. 10m. 4s. = Local apparent time of rising (A.M.)

62. Equation of Time

This is the difference between Mean Time and Apparent Time. Equation of time is the value expressed in time of the angle between the declination circles of the true and mean Sun. We obtain by the above methods the apparent time of sunrise. For this must be applied the equation of time in order to get the mean time, *i.e.*,

Equation of time = Mean Time − Apparent Time at any moment.

(*vice versa* if A.T. is > M.T.)

The equation of time at a moment is positive or negative according as the apparent time is less or greater than mean time.

63. Method of the Determination of Equation of Time to get Mean Time from Apparent Time

From any ephemeris find the Sidereal Time and the Longitude (Sayana) of the Sun for G.M.N. or the G.M.T. corresponding to the approximate time of sunrise or sunset at the required place, on the required date. Find the Sidereal Time at which this particular degree (of Sun's Sayana Longitude referred to above) is on the cusp of the 10th house of

Greenwich or any place. This will give the right ascension expressed in time of the Sun ; or we shall call this, for the sake of convenience, the Sun Time. Take the difference between the Sidereal Time and the Sun Time, and this represents the Equation of Time.*

If the Sun Time is less than the Sidereal Time, the Equation of Time must be subtracted from the Apparent Time (of sunrise or of sunset) in order to obtain the Local Mean Time of rising or of setting. If the Sidereal Time is less than Sun Time, add the Equation of Time for obtaining the Local Mean Time.

Example 10.—*Find the Equation of Time on 16th October 1918, as applied to apparent time at sunrise at Bangalore.*

Approximate time of sunrise = 6 A.M.
 = 12h. 49m. 40s (A.M.) G.M.T.

Sayana Longitude of Sun at G.M.N.
On October 15, was	= 21° 45′ 46″ Libra
On October 16	= 22 45 19

Sun's Sayana Long. at 49m. 40s.
A.M. (G.M.T.) on 16th Oct. = 22 17 35

	H.	M.	S.
When 22° Libra is on the cusp of the tenth house Sidereal Time	= 13	21	20
When 23° Libra is on the cusp of the tenth house Sidereal Time	= 13	25	6

---
* It will do if the Equation of Time is found out for G.M.N

Equation of Time

∴ When 22° 17' 35" Libra is on
the cusp of the tenth house

		H.	M.	S.
the Sidereal Time	=	13	22	28
∴ Sun Time	=	13	22	28
Sidereal Time at (G.M.T.)	=	13	36	10
∴ Equation of Time	= −	0	13	42

Equation of Time at sunrise in the above given place, on October 16, *i.e.*, at 12-50 A.M. (G.M.T.) was : − 14m.

This must be subtracted from the apparent time of sunrise in order to get the Mean Time of sunrise. We subtract this because Sidereal Time is greater than Sun Time.

Example 11.—*Find the Equation of Time on 7th January 1932, as applied to apparent time of sunrise at Dacca.*

Approximate time of sunrise = 6 A.M. = 12 midnight (G.M.T.)

Sayana Longitude of Sun at
G.M.N. on 7th January = 15° 50' 36" Capricorn
∴ Sayana Longitude of Sun
at G.M.T. = 15° 29' 1"

		H.	M.	S.
When 15° Capricorn is on the cusp of the 10th house Sidereal Time	=	19	5	8
When 16° Capricorn is on the cusp of the 10th house Sidereal Time	=	19	9	26
∴ When 15° 29' 1" = Sidereal Time	=	19	7	13
∴ Sun Time	=	19	7	13
Sidereal Time (G.M.T.)	=	19	0	48
∴ Equation of Time at sunrise in the above given place on 7th January, at 12 A.M. (G.M.T.) was	+	0	6	25
			+ 6m.	

This must be added to the Apparent Time of sunrise in order to get the Mean Time of sunrise. We add this because Sun Time is greater than Sidereal Time.

64. The Mean Time of Sunrise and Sunset

Add or subtract the equation of time to or from the apparent time (of sunrise or of sunset). The respective mean time is obtained. The equation of time is positive (*i.e.*, must be added to the apparent time) if the Sun Time (see Article 55) is greater than Sidereal Time and is negative (*i.e.*, must be subtracted from the apparent time) if the Sun Time is less than Sidereal Time.

Example 12.—*Find the Mean Time of sunrise on October 16th, 1918 A.D. at a place on 13° N. Lat. and 5h. 10m. and 20s. E. Long.*

	H.	M.
The apparent time of sunrise was	6	8 A.M. (Ex. 8)
The equation of time (as applied to apparent time at sunrise) was	−0	14 (Table III)
∴ the mean time of sunrise on October 16th was	5	54 A.M.

Example 13.—*Find the Mean Time of sunrise on 7th January 1932 at a place on 36° N. Lat. and 6 hours E. Long.*

	H.	M.
The apparent time of sunrise was	7	10 A.M. (Ex. 9)
The equation of time (as applied to apparent time of sunrise) was	+0	6 (Table III)
∴ the mean time of sunrise there on 7th January was	7	16 A.M.

65. Easy Method for Finding the Mean Time of Sunrise and of Sunset

I have elaborately discussed in the above pages the method of calculating the Apparent Time of sunrise and of sunset for any place on any day, with suitable examples according to both the Hindu and modern systems and the determination of Equation of Time (as applied to the apparent time of sunrise or of sunset) in order to obtain the Mean Time of local sunrise or of sunset. I leave it to the discretion of the reader to choose the method he best prefers.

Those who are not familiar with the method of consulting the Trigonometrical and Logarithmic Tables, a knowledge of which is essential for applying modern methods, may adopt the following rules:—

1. Calculate the Apparent Time of sunrise and of sunset according to the Hindu method (as given in Article 60).
2. Then instead of working out the problem for ascertaining the equation of time, the reader may conveniently find out the Equation of Time by referring to Table III, given at the end of the book.
3. Then apply this Equation of Time to get the Mean Time of sunrise and of sunset by adopting the rules contained in Article 63.
4. Table V gives Mean Times of sunrise and of sunset for different latitudes.

CHAPTER VI

Measures and Conversion of Time

66. Hindu Chronology

The division of time is peculiar to the Hindu. It begins with a Tatpara and ends in a Kalpa (equal to 4,320,000,000 Sidereal years). The Hindu day (an apparent solar day) begins from sunrise and ends with the sunrise. The division of time is thus—

60 Tatparas	=	1 Para
60 Paras	=	1 Vilipta
60 Viliptas	=	1 Lipta
60 Liptas	=	1 Vighati
60 Vighatis	=	1 Ghati
60 Ghatis	=	1 Day

I shall also introduce to the readers the three kinds of days in vogue, though it is not worthwhile wasting any time over remembering them.

(a) **Sidereal Day.**—This is equal to 23h. and 56m. of Mean Solar Time. This is known as *Nakshatra Dina* among the Hindus and this is the time the earth takes to rotate once with reference to any fixed star.

(b) **Apparent Solar Day.**—This is known as the *Savana Dina*. This is longer than the Sidereal day by about four minutes.

Hindu Chronology

According to *Suryasiddhanta* the Savana day is reckoned from sunrise to sunrise.

(c) **Mean Solar Day.**—This is reckoned by considering the average length of all the days in a year.

Two kinds of months are generally in vogue among the Hindus, *viz.*, Chandramana and Souramana. The Chandramana is based upon the movements of the Moon in the celestial circle. The lunar month has 30 lunar days or Tithis. It is the Moon's synodic period from New Moon to New Moon. The solar month is the time, the Sun takes to move in one sign. The month varies in duration according to the number of days the Sun takes to move in a sign. When the Sun enters into the new sign during the course of the lunation, the month is intercalary (Adhika Masa) and is baptised by the name of that which precedes or succeeds it with some prefix to distinguish it from the regular month.

The Hindus have a solar rather sidereal year, which is their astronomical year, and a lunar year which is their civil year.

The lengths of the various years are as follows according to modern calculations :

	D.	H.	M.	S.
The Tropical year	365	5	48	45.6
The Sidereal year	365	6	9	9.7
The Anomalistic year	365	6	13	48

According to *Suryasiddhanta*, the length of the

solar year (sidereal) is 365 days, 15 ghatis, 31 paras and 4 tatparas (365d. 6h. 12m. and 36s. 56) whereas according to *Siddhanta Siromani*, the length of the solar (sidereal) year is 365 days, 5 ghatis, 30 paras and 22.5 tatparas (365d. 6h. 12m. and 9s.). The Savana year has 360 days, the lunar year has 354 days and the Nakshatra (sidereal) year has 324 days.

67. Local Mean Time

The Local mean time of birth is very essential for the calculation of the horoscope. When the Sun is crossing the meridian of any place, it is twelve o'clock or midday at that place according to "Local time". It is noon of local time on any day when the Sun reaches its highest point in the day. It is to be specially noted that the time shown by clocks and watches at any particular day is hardly the correct local mean time. Such times are subject to rectification by observing the course of events in one's life. Great care should be taken to see that watches and clocks, from which birth times are recorded, are accurate. Therefore, the first thing is to ascertain the correct local mean time of birth. The local mean time of a place depends upon its longitude, evidently terrestrial. In all Hindu astrological calculations the meridian of Ujjain was being taken when reckoning time or longitude, but now Greenwich is taken as the centre for such purposes. The local time of a place (L.M.T.), say 4 degrees east of

Local Mean Time

Greenwich, will be 16 minutes later than Greenwich Mean Time (G.M.T.). In other words, if it is 12 noon at Greenwich, it will be 12h. 4m. (P.M.) in a place 1° E. to it, 11-56 A.M. in a place 1° W. to it and so on.

To reduce longitude into time, simply divide the number of degrees, minutes, etc., by 15 and the quotient will be the time. For instance, the longitude of Bangalore is 77° 35′ East of Greenwich. Dividing this by 15 we get 5h. 10m. 20s. The place being East of Greenwich, it will be 5h. 10m. 20s. (P.M.) at Bangalore—(otherwise termed as L.M.T.) when it is noon at Greenwich or 8h. 10m. 20s. (P.M.) when it is 3 P.M. at Greenwich and so on.

The local mean time can be obtained by adding to or subtracting from the Greenwich Mean Time, four minutes to every degree of longitude, according as the place is East or West of Greenwich.

The L.M.T. always synchronises with the G.M.T.

L.M.T. = G.M.T. $\pm$ *Longitude* $\div 15°$

+ if the place is East of Greenwich.
− if the place is West of Greenwich.

Example 14.—*What is the L.M.T. of a place at long. 78° W. when it is 12 noon at Greenwich ?*

$$L.M.T. = 12 \text{ noon} - \frac{78°}{15°} = 12 \text{ noon} - 5h. 12m.$$

= 6h. 48m. (A.M.)

(− because place is West of Greenwich).

68. Standard Time

It is usual to choose for each country, or for each part of a large country, a standard time for use over the whole country. This standard time, as a rule, is the local time of some most important town in the country. If the birth is recorded in L.M.T., well and good ; otherwise, the standard time of the country must be converted into local mean time. The years when standard times were introduced into different countries must be ascertained (see Table IV) In India, standard time was introduced on 1-1-1906 and it is 5h. and 30m. past (in advance) of Greenwich Mean Time. Before this the Madras Time was the adopted Standard Time of the whole of India, and so the standard time of that period should be increased by 9 minutes to obtain the present I.S.T. (*i.e.*, after 1-1-1906). For births that have occurred after 1-1-1906, if the time is recorded in standard time it must be converted into L.M.T. Generally our clocks show standard time. For instance Bangalore is 5h. 10m. 20s. East of Greenwich; when it is noon at Greenwich the L.M.T. at Bangalore is 5h. 10m. 20s. (P.M.) whilst the clock at this time shows 5h. 30m. P.M. (Standard Time).

L.M.T. = Standard Time ± Difference between local and standard longitudes (expressed in time).

+ if local longitude is > Standard Longitude.
− If local longitude is <   do.

69. The Standard Horoscope

In order to illustrate the various principles described in this book, we shall consider the nativity of a female born on 16th October 1918 A.D. at 2h. 26m. P.M. (Indian Standard Time) at a place on 12° 59′ N. Lat. and 77° 34′ E. Long. This horoscope will henceforth be termed as the Standard Horoscope.

Example 15.—*Find the Local Mean Time of birth in the Standard Horoscope, the standard Long. being 82° 30′ East of Greenwich (5h. 30m. ahead of G.M.T.)*

Standard Longitude = 82° 30′
Local Longitude = 77° 34′

Difference between Std. Long.
and Local Long. = 4° 56′

4° 56′ = 19m. 44s. in time.

∴ Local Longitude is < Standard Longitude, this time must be subtracted from the Standard Time.

∴ L.M.T. = 2h. 26m. − 19m. 44s. = 2h. 6m. 16s. (P.M.)
∴ L.M.T. of Birth = 2-6-16 (P.M.)

70. Suryodayadi Jananakala Ghatikaha

It is customary among the Hindus to mention the time of birth as "Suryodayadi Jananakala Ghatikaha", *i.e.*, the number of ghatis passed from sunrise upto the moment of birth. First ascertain the local mean time of birth and of sunrise and then apply the following rule :

(24 seconds = 1 vighati ; 24 minutes = 1 ghati; 1 hour = 2½ ghatis)

(Birth Time − Sunrise) × 2½ = Suryodayadi Jananakala Ghatikaha.

Example 16.—*Find the Suryodayadi Jananakala Ghatikaha in the Standard Horoscope.*

Sunrise (L.M.T.) = 5–53–40 A.M. on 16th October 1918.
Birth time (L.M.T.) = 2–6–16 P.M.

∴ (2–6–16 P.M.) − 5–53–40 × $2\frac{1}{2}$ = Gh. 20–$31\frac{1}{2}$

∴ Suryodayadi Jananakala Ghatikaha
(Number of ghatis passed from sunrise
upto birth)   = Gh 20–$31\frac{1}{2}$ or 20–32.

Example 17.—*Miss G. born on 24-10-1949 at 3-13 p.m. (L.M.T.), Lat. 13° N. and Long. 5h. 10m. and 20s. E. Find Suryodayadi Jananakala Ghatikaha.*

Sunrise (L.M.T.)   = 5–52 A.M.
Birth Time (L.M.T.) = 3–13 P.M.

∴ Suryodayadi Jananakala Ghatikaha = 23–38

CHAPTER VII

Graha Sphutas

(PLANETARY LONGITUDES)

71. The Hindu Almanac

It requires a considerable amount of familiarity with the advanced portions of astronomical principles, in order to find out the longitudes of planets independently, *i.e.*, without reference to any almanac. As such I have reserved discretion to expound those principles in a separate book, and for the present, simply describe the method commonly adopted by all astrological students and adepts. Any reliable almanac will serve our purpose. There are still a few standard *Panchangas* (almanacs) which can be trusted for astrological purposes.

72. Method of Making Graha Sphutas

If the panchanga is available for the place of birth then no trouble of conversion of time is involved ; otherwise, birth time must be converted into local time of the place, for which the almanac is calculated, in order to find out the planetary positions.

Find out the date of birth in the almanac and note down all the details given for that day. If no planets are marked on the day of birth then trace back and find out the position of the planet on the date, nearest to that of birth. It will be found that the planet's position will have been marked in Nakshatras (constellations) and Padas (quarters) with time of entry in ghatis into the particular pada. Find out the time at which the same planet enters the next quarter of the constellation. Mark the interval in ghatis between the entries of the planet into these two quarters. Mark also the interval between the first entry and the birth time and proceed as follows :—

Formula (a) **for all Planets :**

$$\frac{\text{The interval between the first entry and birth}}{\text{The interval between the two entries}} \times 3\tfrac{1}{2}$$

= The number of degrees traversed in that particular quarter of the nakshatra.

Formula (b) **for the Moon:**

$$\frac{\text{The interval between entry into the first degree of the sign and birth}}{\text{Time taken for traversing the sign}} \times 30°$$

Add this to the number of degrees the planet has at the time of the first entry. Its Nirayana Longitude is obtained.

Example 18.—*Find the Nirayana Longitudes of the planets in the Standard Horoscope.*

The Almanac for 1918 gives the following information :
15-10-1918. Sun enters 3rd quarter of Chitta at 25-28 Gh.
18-10-1918.   Do.   4th quarter   do.   at 46-53 do.
Therefore the period taken by the Sun to pass through one pada or 3 1/3 degrees of the celestial arc is :—

Planetary Longitudes

	Gh.	Vig.
15th October	34	32 (Subtract the time of entry from 60 Gh. being the duration of a day)
16th ,,	60	0
17th ,,	60	0
18th ,,	46	53
Total Gh.	201	25 or Vighatis 12,085.

Time elapsed from the entry of the Sun into the 3rd quarter of Chitta (which is nearest to the birth, upto the movement of birth):

	Gh.	Vig.
15th October	34	32
16th ,,	20	32
Total Gh.	55	4 or Vig. 3,304.

Apply formula (a) :—The arc traversed by the Sun = $\frac{3304}{12085} \times 3\frac{1}{3}° = 0° 55'$.

This distance, the Sun has passed in the third pada or quarter of Chitta. We know that the last two quarters of Chitta, the four of Swati and the first three of Visakha constitute Thula (Libra).

∴ The Nirayana longitude of the Sun = 0° 55' in Libra
= 180° 55' from the 1st degree of Aries.

THE MOON

	Gh.	Vig.
14-10-1918 : Duration of Sravana =	59	21
∴ Dhanishta lasts for	0	39 (Subtracting 59-21 from 60)
15-10-1918 Do.	57	14
∴ Duration of Dhanishta	57	53
15-10-1918 Satabhisha lasts for	2	46 (Subtracting 57-14 from 60)

16-10-1918 Satabhisha lasts for   54   19

∴ Duration of Satabhisha   57   5

16-10-1918 Poorvabhadra lasts for   5   41   (Subtracting 54-19 from 60)

17-10-1918   do.   50   48

∴ Duration of Poorvabhadra   56   29

Aquarius is made up of : last 2 quarters of Dhanishta *plus* Satabhisha *plus* 3 quarters of Poorvabhadra.

$= \frac{1}{2}(57-53) + (57-5) + \frac{3}{4}(56-29) =$ Gh. 128-23

i.e., The Moon takes Gh. 128-23 to travel through the sign of Aquarius.

The interval between the Moon's entry into the first degree of Aquarius and birth time is found as follows :—

$\frac{1}{2}(57-53) + (20-31\frac{1}{2}) =$ Gh. 49-28

Applying formula (*b*)

$= \frac{\text{Gh. } 49-29}{\text{Gh. } 128-23} \times 30° = 11° 33' 33''$ in Aquarius.

Moon's Nirayana position is 11° 33' 33'' in Aquarius.

i.e., 311° 33' 33'' from the first degree of Aries.

Note :— The actual ephemerical position is 311° 12' 19''.

73. Nirayana Longitude of Planets

The Longitudes of other planets, similarly found out, are reproduced below for ready reference.

Graha (Planet)	Sphuta (Longitude)
The Sun	180° 55'
The Moon	311 19
Mars	229 29
Mercury	181 33
Jupiter	84 3
Venus	171 12

Graha (Planet)	Sphuta (Longitude)
Saturn	124° 25'
Rahu	234 31
Ketu	54 31

Explanation : The above positions have been calculated on the basis of a panchanga. Therefore they can be said to be *fairly* correct. Positions obtained from modern ephemerides (*vide* Chapter XI) should be considered accurate.

CHAPTER VIII

Lagna Sphuta
(THE ASCENDANT)

74. Lagna or Ascendant

Lagna or the ascendant is that point of the ecliptic, which at any time is on the eastern horizon. It is expressed in signs, degrees, etc., of Stellar Aries.

75. Solar Months

The earth is egg-shaped and rotates once in a day on its axis from west to east, and thus, all the zodiacal signs are invariably exposed to the solar influence. The twelve solar months are named after the twelve zodiacal signs. On the first day of Aries the first degree of that particular sign is at the eastern horizon, and the remaining signs are gradually exposed till the next day when at the sunrise, the second degree of Aries will be at the eastern horizon. The sunrise takes place in the last degree of the zodiac on the 30th day of Pisces when the solar year closes, *i.e.*, the Lagna is that particular place or point which is on the eastern horizon at any particular time. The sunrise determines the Udaya Lagna and the degree and the sign, in which the Sun rises, will be the ascendant at that moment. Lagna is the eastern point of the ecliptic where it meets the horizon.

76. Determination of Lagna

First find out the true Nirayana position of the Sun and add the Ayanamsa to it so that the Sun's Sayana Longitude is obtained. Ascertain the sign of the ecliptic the Sun is in; the degrees he has traversed in it and those he has yet to pass through. The number of degrees he has gained are the Bhukthamsas, and those to cover, the Bhogyamsas. Now from the *Rasimanas* of the place, find out the *Bhogya Kala*, *i.e.*, the time required to pass through the Bhogyamsas, thus:

Formula (a)—

$$\frac{\text{Period of rising sign where the Sayana Sun is}}{30°} \times \text{Bhogyamsa}$$

$$= \text{Bhogya Time}$$

Now from the *Ishta Kala* (the time for which the Lagna is required) subtract the Bhogya time. From the remainder subtract the periods of rising of the next and successive signs as long as you can. Finally you will find the sign, the rising period of which being greater than the remainder, you will not be able to subtract any more. Consequently this is called the Ashuddha sign and its rising period, the Ashuddha rising. It is evident that the Ashuddha sign is of course on the horizon at the given time. The degrees of the Ashuddha sign, which are above the horizon, are the passed degrees and hence called the Bhuktha—are thus found :

Formula (b)—

$$\frac{30°}{\text{Rising period of the Ashuddha sign}} \times \text{The ramainder of given time}$$
= Passed degrees of the Ashuddha sign

Add to these passed degrees so determined, the preceding signs reckoned from the first point of Aries and from the total, subtract the Ayanamsa. The remainder represents the Lagna from the Stellar Aries.

Example 19.—*Find the Lagna in the Standard Horoscope* :

Nirayana Long. of the Sun	...	180° 55′ 0″	
Ayanamsa	... +	21° 16′ 41″	
Sayana Long. of the Sun		202° 11′ 41″	

i.e., the Sayana Sun is in Libra 22° 11′ 41″.

∴ Bhukthamsas (passed degrees) = 22° 11′ 41″ or 22° 12′ in Libra.

∴ Bhogyamsas (degrees yet to pass) = 7° 48′ in Libra,

∴ Bhogya Time = $\frac{7° 48'}{30°}$ × Gh. 5–6 = Gh. 1–17½

i.e., the Sun has to traverse in Libra for Gh. 1–17½
Scorpio ... 2–10⅚
Sagittarius ... 5–30⅔
Capricorn ... 5–13

Total ... Gh. 17–22

		Gh.	Vig.
Ishta Kala	=	20	31½
Ghatis passed till the end of Capricorn	=	17	22
Bhuktha period in the Ashuddha sign, *viz.*, Aquarius		Gh. 3	9½

Bhukthamsas

The Bhukthamsas correspond to the above Bhuktha time:
Applying—

Formula $(b) = \dfrac{30°}{\text{Gh. } 4\text{-}37\frac{1}{2}} \times \text{Gh. } 3\text{-}9\frac{1}{2} = 20° \ 29' \ 20''$

(Aquarius).

∴ The Sayana Lagna   = 20° 29′ 20″
   Less Ayanamsa   = 21° 16′ 41″
∴ The true Lagna   29 12 39
                      or 29° 13′.

The Lagna of Standard Horoscope is 29° 13′, Makara or Capricorn: or converting this into degrees,[*] it is 299° 13′ from the first point of Stellar Aries.

Now adding 180° to this, viz., the Udaya Lagna, the Asta Lagna (Descendant) is obtained.

77. Rasi Kundali

This is the zodiacal diagram representing a picture of the heavens at the time of birth. The diagram given below is the one generally in vogue in South India.

♓	♈	♉ Ketu	☐ Jupiter
♒ Moon	\multicolumn{2}{c}{MAP OF THE HEAVENS}	♋
♑ Ascdt.			♌ Saturn
♐	♍ Mars Rahu	♎ Merc. Sun	♏ Venus

[*] The correct Longitude of Lagna is 28° 27′ in Nirayana Capricorn as per calculations based on modern astronomical ephemerides—see also Chapter XI.

CHAPTER IX

Dasama Bhava Sphuta

(TENTH HOUSE OR THE MID-HEAVEN)

78. The Dasama Bhava

This is also known as the Madhya Lagna. It is on the correct determination of this that the entire fabric of the horoscope rests. In fact, all the other Bhavas (Houses) are very easily arrived at, after the longitude of the Dasama Bhava has been definitely ascertained. In the astronomical language, the Madhya Lagna may be described as the culminating point of the ecliptic on the meridian. Astrologically speaking, the Dasama Bhava plays a very important part in the profession, rather the means of livelihood of a person—otherwise known as *Karma*.

79. Rasi Chakra

A broad distinction must be mentioned between the Rasi Chakra (see Art. 77) and the Bhava Chakra (see Art. 82) so that the reader does not mistake the one for the other. The Rasi Chakra is simply a figure of the fixed zodiac with the limits and occupants of its 12 signs as well as Lagna clearly marked. Each sign is just one-twelfth part of the zodiac made up of 30 ecliptic degrees.

80. Conception of Bhava Chakra

The conception prevalent amongst some astrologers that the Rasi Chakra and the Bhava Chakra are the same is erroneous. After the Lagna Sphuta (longitude of the ascendant) has been determined, the limits and durations of other Bhavas have to be ascertained. In India, there are two schools of thought bearing on the question of Bhava Sphutas (house-division). According to one view, shared by a vast majority of people not only in India but also in Europe and America, the length of each Bhava will be 30 degrees—the influence extending 15 degrees on either side of the ascending degree (equal house system). According to the other view, this system is unscientific because it ignores the relationship between the ecliptic and equator which should be considered for determining the dimensions of the Bhavas. Classical writers like Sripathi favour the determination of Bhavas on the lines given in the following paragraphs. In our own humble experience extending for nearly 35 years the equal house system appears to yield more satisfactory results. The student of astrology need not concern himself with such controversial issues. He may safely follow the Sripathi (known in the West as Porphyry method), expounded in the following pages.

81. Bhaskara's Definition

Bhaskaracharya describes a Bhava Chakra thus: "The point where the ecliptic cuts the horizon in the

East is known as the Rising Lagna, and the point where the ecliptic cuts the horizon in the west is known as the Setting Lagna and the points where the meridian of the place cuts the ecliptic are known as the Zenith Lagna (above the earth) and the Nadir Lagna (below the earth)."

82. Bhava Chakra

This is an unequal marking of the ecliptic into twelve divisions (Houses) with reference to the latitude of the place and the moment of birth (See next chapter for the definition of a House). The Bhava Sphuta involves elaborate processes such as the determination of the limits—cusps of the various *Bhavas* (Houses)—comprehended as *Bhava Sandhis* and other details connected with them which form the subject-matter of the succeeding chapter.

83. Method of Determination of the Mid-heaven

The interval between the midday and the time of the day indicated by the position of the Sun is termed as *Natha*, *i.e.*, the meridian distance. This Natha may be either *Prag*, *i.e.*, eastern or *Paschad*, *i.e.*, western. It is *Prag* between midnight and midday and *Paschad* between midday and midnight. The *Pragnatha* comprehends to condition, *viz.* :

(1) the distance between the Sun and the Meridian when the birth occurs after sunrise, and
(2) the distance between the Meridian and the Sun when the birth occurs before sunrise,

Determination of Sunrise

i.e., when the Sun is still below the eastern horizon.

Similarly the *Paschadnatha* also includes two conditions, *viz.*:

(1) the distance between the Meridian and the Sun if the birth occurs before sunset, and

(2) the distance between the Meridian and the Sun after he has set. Natha when subtracted from 30 ghatis gives *Unnatha*.

Here it must be noted that the Meridian refers to apparent noon and the Sun refers to the birth time.

After clearly understanding the meaning and significance of the words Natha and Unnatha, ascertain, if the birth has fallen in Pragnatha, or Paschadnatha: in Pragnatha,

(a) if the birth has occurred after sunrise, deduct the birth time (in ghatis) from *Dinardha* (half diurnal duration);

(b) if it has occurred before sunrise, add *Dinardha* to the ghatis elapsed from the birth time up to sunrise.

The result in both the cases is Pragnatha, *i.e.*, Pragnatha is indicated by the time, elapsed between birth moment and local apparent noon. In Paschadnatha,

(a) If the birth has taken place in the afternoon and before sunset, deduct *Dinardha* from the birth time (in ghatis);

(b) if the birth has occurred after sunset, add *Dinardha* to the interval between sunset and birth moment; the duration of Paschadnatha is obtained.

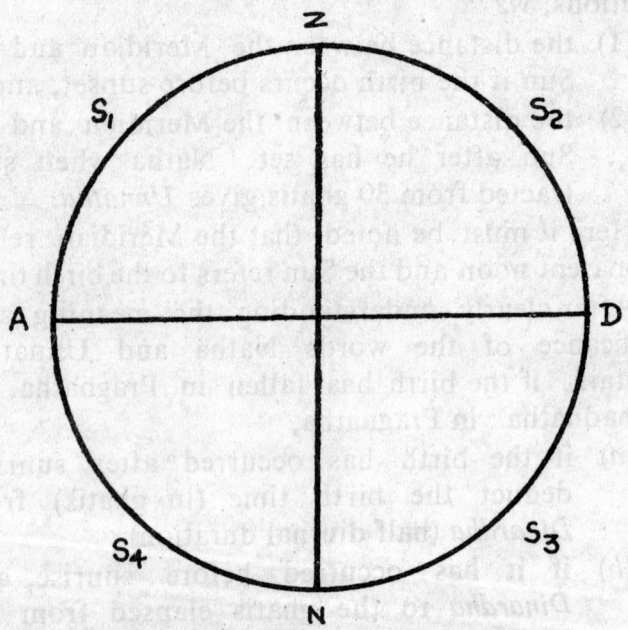

S₁, S₂, S₃, S₄ REPRESENT SUN'S POSITIONS
A = Ascendant (Udaya Lagna)
Z = Zenith or Meridian (Madhya Lagna)
D = Descendant (Asta Lagna)
N = Nadir (Patala Lagna)

Natha = Distance from S₁ to Z ⎱ Both are Pragnatha
      =   ,,   ,,   S₄ to Z ⎰
      =   ,,   ,,   Z to S₂ ⎱ Paschadnatha
         ,,   ,,   Z to S₃ ⎰

Mid-Heaven Determination

The above observations may be summarised thus:—

Rule 1—**When Birth is between Midnight and Midday:**
(a) Dinardha − Suryodayadi Jananakala Ghatikaha = Pragnatha Period.
(b) Dinardha + interval between birth and sunrise = Pragnatha Period.

Rule 2—**When Birth is between Midday and Midnight:**
(a) Suryodayadi Jananakala Ghatikaha − Dinardha = Paschadnatha Period.
(b) Dinardha + interval between sunset and birth = Paschadnatha Period.

Rule 3—30 Ghatis − Natha = Unnatha

Example 20.—*Find the nature of the Natha and its duration in the Standard Horoscope.*

It comes under "birth between midday and midnight" and Rule 2 (a) can be applied to it as the birth has occurred after midday and before sunset.

Dinardha (half diurnal duration) = Gh. 14 Vig. 42
Birth Time = Gh. 20 Vig. $31\frac{1}{2}$.
∴ Gh. 20 Vig. $31\frac{1}{2}$ − Gh. 14 Vig. 42 = Gh. 5 Vig. $49\frac{1}{2}$
∴ Nature of Natha = Paschad.
Its duration = Gh. 5-$49\frac{1}{2}$* or 5-50.

Example 21.—*What is the Unnatha period in a case in which Pragnatha = 17 Ghatis?*

Applying Rule 3 we get
(Gh. 30 − Gh. 17 = Gh. 13 = Period of Unnatha)

From the position of the Sayana Sun and reckoning the rising periods on the equator, find out

---
* Natha is simply the interval between the Mean Time of Apparent Noon and Mean Time of Birth. In this case the interval is L.M.T. of Birth (2-6 P.M.)−M.T. of Apparent Noon (11-46 A.M.) = 2h. 20m. = Gh.5-50.

the arc (in the reverse order) that corresponds to the Natha period. Add this to or subtract from Sayana Sun according as the Natha is Paschad or Prag. The result, diminished by Ayanamsa, gives Nirayana Madhya Lagna.

Example 22.—*Deduce Nirayana Madhya Lagna in the Standard Horoscope.*

Paschadnatha = Gh. 5-50 (Ex. 20).

Sayana Sun = 202° 11′ 41″ = Libra 22° 11′ 41″.

The rising period of 22° 11′ 41″ in Libra at the equator

$$= \frac{22° \ 11' \ 41''}{30°} \times \text{Gh. 4-39} = \text{Gh. 3-26}\tfrac{1}{2}$$

Reckoning in the reverse direction, we find that Gh. 3 Vig. 26½ are passed in Libra.

In Virgo have passed, Natha — Gh. 3 Vig. 26½ or Gh. 5 Vig. 50 − Gh. 3 Vig. 26½ = Gh. 2-23½.

∴ Arc corresponding to Gh. 2 Vig. 23½ Virgo (on the equator)

$$= \frac{\text{Gh. 2 Vig. 23}\tfrac{1}{2}}{\text{Gh. 4 Vig. 39}} \times 30° = 15° \ 22' \ 33' \tfrac{26''}{31}$$

$$= 15° \ 22' \ 34''$$

∴ The distance between the Sun and Meridian is :

Libra	....	22°	11′	41″
Virgo	....	15°	22′	34″
Meridian distance	....	37°	34′	15″

Since the Natha is Paschad, add this to Sayana Sun.

Sayana Sun	....	202°	11′	41″
Meridian distance	....	37°	34′	15″
∴ Sayana Madhya Lagna	....	239°	45′	56″
Less Ayanamsa	....	21°	15′	57″
∴ Nirayana Madhya Lagna		218°	29′	59″
	=	218°	30′	

Mid-Heaven Determination

∴ The Mid-heaven or
Madhya Lagna* = 218° 30'
= Scorpio 8° 30'

In other words, this is the Longitude of the Bhava Madhya or the middle point of the tenth house.

---

* Based on the modern trigonometrical calculations the longitude of mid-heaven will be 216° 37'. In the Standard Horoscope modern values alone have been adopted.

CHAPTER X

Bhava Sphutas
(LONGITUDES OF HOUSES)

84. Bhava or House

According to the Hindus a Bhava means one-third of the arc of the ecliptic intercepted between any two adjacent angles, *viz.*, the Udaya Lagna (Eastern Horizon), the Patala Lagna (Lower Meridian), the Asta Lagna (Western Horizon), and the Madhya Lagna (Upper Meridian).

85. Bhava Madhyas

The points of trisection of the ecliptic arcs referred to above are the *Bhava Madhyas* or the mid-points of the Bhavas.

86. Kendra Bhavas

These are the four angular houses in a horoscope, *viz.*, the Udaya Lagna, the Patala Lagna, the Asta Lagna and the Madhya Lagna (Article 83). They are considered very important astrologically.

87. Determination of Kendra Bhavas

The preceding two chapters deal exhaustively with the method of determining the Ascendant and the Mid-heaven—two of the Kendra Bhavas. The

Asta Lagna (descendant or Western Horizon) and the Patala or Rasatala Lagna (Lower Meridian) are determined thus:—

Rule 1.—Udaya Lagna (Ascendant or East Horizon) + 180°
= Asta Lagna (Descendant or West Horizon).

Rule 2.—Madhya Lagna + 180° = Rasatala Lagna.
(Upper Meridian) + 180° = (Lower Meridian).

Example 23.—*Determine the Longitudes of the Asta Lagna and Patala Lagna in the Standard Horoscope.*

$$\text{Udaya Lagna} = 298° \; 27'$$
$$\text{Madhya Lagna} = 216° \; 36'$$

(Applying Rule 1)

∴ 298° 27' + 180° = 118° 27' (Expunge 360°)

(Applying Rule 2)

∴ 216° 36' + 180° = 36° 36' (Expunge 360°)

∴ Asta Lagna = 118° 27'.

Patala = 36° 36'.

88. Non-Angular Houses

These are the houses between the angular ones. For instance, angular houses are the I (Eastern Horizon)—IV (Lower Meridian)—VII (Western Horizon)—and X (Upper Meridian). The rest, *viz.*, II, III, V, VI, VIII, IX, XI and XII are the non-angular houses otherwise known as the Panapara Bhavas (Succeedent Houses), and the Apoklima Bhavas (Cadent Houses)—see Articles 22 and 23. The Madhyas of these Bhavas are the points of trisection referred to above (Articles 83 and 84).

89. Determination of Bhava Madhyas of Non-angular Houses

There are four angles in a Bhava Chakra.

First ascertain—rather determine the ecliptic arcs between these four angles, *viz.*, (*a*) the arc between the Eastern Horizon and the Lower Meridian; (*b*) between the Lower Meridian and the Western Horizon; (*c*) between the Western Horizon and Upper Meridian; and (*d*) between the Upper Meridian and the Eastern Horizon.

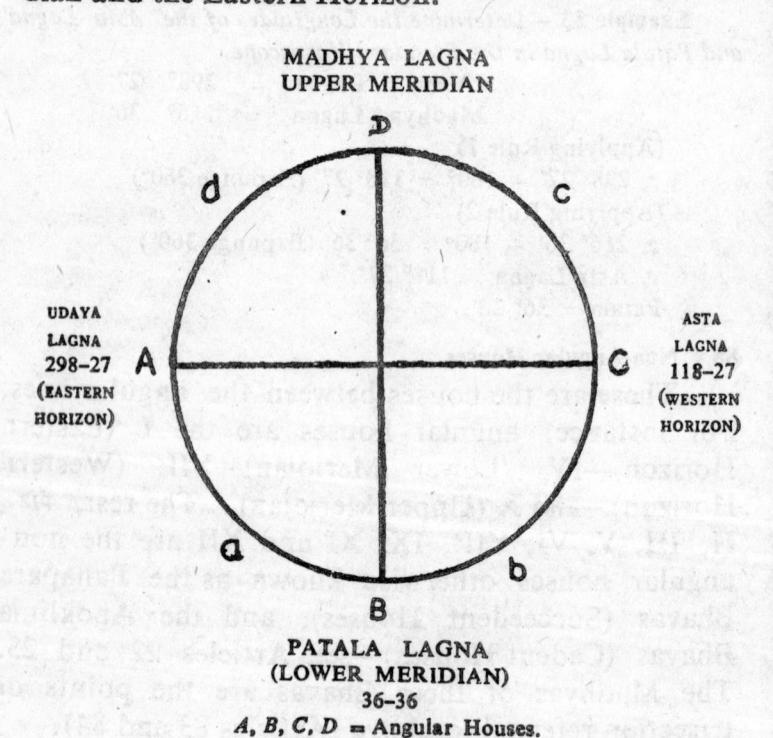

MADHYA LAGNA
UPPER MERIDIAN

UDAYA LAGNA
298-27
(EASTERN HORIZON)

ASTA LAGNA
118-27
(WESTERN HORIZON)

PATALA LAGNA
(LOWER MERIDIAN)
36-36

A, B, C, D = Angular Houses.
a, b, c, d = Ecliptic arcs.

Non-Angular Houses

Trisect each arc: For instance, trisect arc a. The result is $1/3a = a/3$. Add this to the Longitude of the Bhava Madhya of the Udaya Lagna and that of the II Bhava (Madhya) is obtained. To the Longitude of the II Bhava add $a/3$; that of the III is obtained. Again trisect arc b. The result would be $b/3$; add $b/3$ to the Longitude of the Lower Meridian; that of the V Bhava is obtained. Similarly deal with the other arcs for obtaining the Madhyas of the rest of the Bhavas. The four arcs may thus be determined.

Arc a = Longitude of Lower Meridian—Longitude of Eastern Horizon.

Arc b = Longitude of Western Horizon—Longitude of Lower Meridian.

Arc c = Longitude of Upper Meridian—Longtiude of Western Horizon.

Arc d = Longitude of Eastern Horizon—Longitude of Upper Meridian.

Example 24.—*Determine the ecliptic arcs between the four angles in the Standard Horoscope.*

Arc a = 36° 36′ — 298° 27′ = 98° 9′
Arc b = 118 27 — 36 36 = 81 51
Arc c = 216 36 — 118 27 = 98   9
Arc d = 298 27 — 216 36 = 81 51

*a = 98   9
 b = 81 51
 c = 98   9
 d = 81 51

Example 25.—*Find the Bhava Madhyas of the Non-angular Houses in the Standard Horoscope.*

Long. of the Udaya Lagna   = 298° 27′
Arc a*   = 98° 9′

---

* Note.—Arc a = c and Arc b = d.

∴ Trisecting arc a, we get :

$$\frac{a}{3} = \frac{98° \ 9'}{3} = 32° \ 43'$$

∴ 298° 27' + 32° 43' = 331° 10' = II Bhava
   331° 10' + 32° 43' = 3° 53' = III Bhava

Long. of Lower Meridian = 36 36'
Arc b = 81° 51'

∴ Trisecting arc b, we get :

$$\frac{b}{2} = \frac{81° \ 51'}{3} = 27° \ 17'$$

∴ 36° 36' + 27° 17' = 63° 53' = V Bhava
  63° 53' + 27° 17' = 91° 10' = VI Bhava

Long. of Western Horizon = 118° 27'
Arc c = 98° 9'
∴ $c/3$ = 32° 43'
∴ 118° 27' + 32° 43' = 151° 10' = VIII Bhava
  151° 10' + 32° 43' = 183° 53' = IX Bhava

Long. of Upper Meridian = 216° 36'
Arc d = 81° 51'
∴ $d/3$ = 27° 17'
∴ 216° 36' + 27° 17' = 243° 53' = XI Bhava
  243° 53' + 27° 17' = 271° 10' = XII Bhava

Example 26.—*Mark the Bhava Sphutas in the Standard Horoscope.*

	Bhava (House)	Sphuta (Longitude)
I	Lagna or the Thanu Bhava	= 298° 27'
II	,, Dhana ,,	= 331 10
III	,, Bhratru ,,	= 3 53
IV	,, Matru ,,	= 36 36
V	,, Putra ,,	= 63 53
VI	,, Satru ,,	= 91 10
VII	,, Kalatra ,,	= 118 27
VIII	,, Ayur ,,	= 151 10

	Bhava (House)		Sphuta (Longitude)
IX	Lagna or the Dharma Bhava	=	183° 53'
X	,, Karma ,,	=	216 36
XI	,, Labha ,,	=	243 53
XII	,, Vraya ,,	=	271 10

90. Bhava Sandhis

These are the junctional points of the two consecutive Bhavas. The potency of a Bhava will be at its full in the Bhava Madhya and hence, it must begin somewhere and end somewhere. The influence of a planet will gradually rise when approaching Bhava Madhya, while it gradually diminishes from Bhava Madhya till it is practically nil at the Bhava Sandhi. The place or the point where the influence of the Bhava begins is the Arambha-sandhi and the place where it ends is the Virama-sandhi. The Arambha-sandhi may be termed as the first point of the house, and the Virama-sandhi, the last point. For instance, the Arambha-sandhi of the first Bhava will be the end-point of the 12th Bhava. Similarly the Virama-sandhi of the first Bhava will be the end point of the Lagna and the Arambha-sandhi of the second house and so on. In other words the sandhi of a Bhava represents the beginning of the influence of one Bhava and termination of the influence of the Bhava preceding it.

In order to know the exact amount of the influence that a planet exercises, as a result of its position in a particular Bhava, it becomes necessary to determine the sandhis of the various Bhavas.

91. Determination of Bhava Sandhis

Add the longitudes of two consecutive Bhavas and divide the sum by 2. The result represents sandhi. For instance, in the Standard Horoscope adding the longitudes of first and second Bhavas and dividing the sum by 2, we get :—

$$\frac{298° 27' + 331° 10'}{2}$$

$$= \frac{629° 37'}{2} = 314° 48' 30''$$

i.e., Aquarius 14° 48′ 30″ is the sandhi-point between the I and II Houses; or the Virama-sandhi of the I Bhava is 314° 48′ 30″ and the Arambha-sandhi of the II Bhava is 314° 48′ 30″. It is sufficient if sandhis for 6 Bhavas are determined as those of the rest (opposite six houses) can be obtained by adding 180° to each of them.

Example 27.—*Find the Longitudes of the Arambha-sandhis of the twelve Bhavas in the Standard Horoscope.*

```
                                          Arambha-sandhi
  I  (271° 19' + 298° 27') ÷ 2 = 284° 41' 30"
 II  (298  27  + 331  10 ) ÷ 2 = 314  48  30
III  (331  10  +   3  53 ) ÷ 2 = 347  31  30
 IV  (  3  53  +  36  36 ) ÷ 2 =  20  14  30
  V  ( 36  36  +  63  53 ) ÷ 2 =  55  14  30
 VI  ( 63  53  +  91  10 ) ÷ 2 =  77  31  30
```

The Arambha, Madhya and Anthya of the Bhavas are thus situated :—

Bhava	Arambha			Madhya		Anthya		
I	284°	48'	30"	298°	27'	314°	48'	30"
II	314	48	30	331	10	347	31	30
III	347	31	30	3	53	20	14	30
IV	20	14	30	36	36	50	14	30
V	50	14	30	63	53	77	31	30
VI	77	31	30	91	10	104	48	30
VII	104	48	30	118	27	134	48	30
VIII	134	48	30	151	10	167	31	30
IX	167	31	30	183	53	200	14	30
X	200	14	30	216	36	230	14	30
XI	230	14	30	243	53	257	31	30
XII	257	31	30	271	10	248	48	30

92. Poorva and Uttara Bhagas of Bhavas

The Poorva Bhaga is that part of the Bhava which first rises and the Uttara Bhaga is the part that next rises. They can be thus determined:

Rule 1.—Poorva Bhaga of a Bhava = Long. of the Bhava Madhya—Long. of the Arambha-sandhi.

Rule 2.—Uttara Bhaga = Long. of Virama-sandhi — Long. of the Bhava Madhya.

Rule 3.—Length of each Bhava = Length of Poorva Bhaga + Length of Uttara Bhaga.

Example 28.—*Find the Poorva and Uttara Bhagas and the length of each Bhava in the Standard Horoscope.*

Applying the above rules we get the following results:—

	Poorva Bhaga of the Bhava			Uttara Bhaga of the Bhava			Length of the Bhava		
I	13°	38'	30"	16°	21'	30"	30°	0'	0"
II	16	21	30	16	21	30	32	43	0
III	16	21	30	16	21	30	32	43	0
IV	16	21	30	13	38	30	30	0	0

	Poorva Bhaga of the Bhava	Uttara Bhaga of the Bhava	Length of the Bhava
V	13° 38′ 30″	13° 38′ 30″	27° 17′ 0″
VI	13 38 30	13 38 30	27 17 0
VII	13 38 30	16 21 30	30 0 0
VIII	16 21 30	16 21 30	32 43 0
IX	16 21 30	16 21 30	32 43 0
X	16 21 30	13 38 30	30 0 0
XI	13 38 30	13 38 30	27 17 0
XII	13 38 30	13 38 30	27 17 0

CHAPTER XI

Casting the Horoscope according to the Western Method and Its Reduction to the Hindu

93. General Observations

Hitherto we have exhaustively treated the processes involved in casting a horoscope according to the Hindu method. Realising the fact that to a number of people who are anxious to apply the Hindu method of astrology, authentic Hindu almanacs are not either accessible or intelligible, we have thought it fit to include a chapter dealing with the method of computing the longitudes of planets, etc., according to modern methods and their reduction to the Hindu.

In view of the fact that ancient Hindu values of durations of the signs, etc., require correction in the light of observations, one has to rely, for purposes of accuracy, on the astronomical constants obtained on the basis of modern trigonometrical methods. Hence, in preference to the methods chalked out in Chapters IX and X, the method of casting horoscopes as per principles given in this chapter may be adopted for greater accuracy. In the standard horoscope, planetary positions and the longitudes of the ascendant and Midheaven, as illustrated in the previous chapter, have been obtained on the basis explained in this chapter.

94. Hindu and Western Methods

The Hindu method of casting a horoscope is always Sayana though finally it is reduced to the Nirayana for predictive purposes, so that, we want Nirayana Longitudes of planets and Bhavas, for analysing a horoscope according to the rules given in books dealing with the *Phalit Bhaga* (judicial portion) of astrology.

The westerners base their calculations as well as predictions on the shifting zodiac, *i.e.*, the longitudes of planets, etc., given by them correspond to those of Sayana amongst us, so that by subtracting the Ayanamsa from such positions, the Nirayana Longitudes can be obtained.

95. The Modern Ephemeris

In order to cast a horoscope according to the western method, a reliable ephemeris must be secured. An ephemeris will contain such information as the longitudes of planets, their latitudes and declinations and the Sidereal Time marked out for each day and calculated to Greenwich Mean Noon. In some, the Equation of Time referred to in the preceding chapters will also be given in addition to the daily motions of planets. A modern ephemeris

G.M.T. of Birth

roughly corresponds to a Hindu almanac with the difference that while the former is exclusively Sayana, among the latter, some are Sayana and besides, a Hindu *Panchanga* contains much useful information like *tithi, yoga, karana*, etc., whose importance, it is out of place to make mention of here, than an ephemeris.

96. *Table of Houses

These are absolutely necessary for ascertaining the ascendant and other Houses knowing beforehand the Sidereal Time at the birth moment. The latitude of the birthplace must be sought for in a "Table of Houses" and then the ascendant, etc., traced for the Sidereal Time. The cusps of the Houses of the western system correspond to the Sayana Bhava Madhyas of the Hindus and by the subtraction of the Ayanamsa, their Nirayana Bhava Madhyas can be obtained.

Cusp of the Western House — Ayanamsa = Nirayana Bhava Madhya of the Hindus.

97. Local Mean Time of Birth

If the birth moment is marked in Standard Time convert it into Local Mean Time (L.M.T.) (See Article 65).

---

* *Nirayana Tables of Houses*, published by Raman Publications, obviates the necessity for reducing Sayana houses into Nirayana and can be employed by all astrological students and savants.

98. Greenwich Mean Time of Birth

As the Sayana longitudes of planets are given for Greenwich Mean Time (G.M.T.) generally for Greenwich Mean Noon (G.M.N.), the L.M.T. of birth must be converted into the corresponding G.M.T. of birth thus :

$$G.M.T. = L.M.T. + \frac{\text{Longitude of place}}{15°}$$

− if place is East of Greenwich.
+ if place is West of Greenwich.

Example 29.—*Birth on 16-10-1918 at 2-6-16 p.m.(L.M.T.) Lat. 13° N , Long. 77° 34' E. Find the G.M.T. of birth.*

$$G.M.T. = 2\text{-}6\text{-}16 \text{ p.m.} \frac{77° \ 34'}{15}$$

2-6-16 p.m. − 5-10-16 = 8-56-0 a.m.

∴ G.M.T. of Birth = 8-56 a.m.

99. Greenwich Mean Time Interval of Birth

As already observed, the longitudes of planets are given for Greenwich Mean Noon (sometimes for midnight also). In order to find out their positions at the moment of birth, we should ascertain the elapsed time, rather the interval between the G.M.N. and the G.M.T. If the G.M.T. of the birth falls after the noon (*i.e.*, G.M.N.) then take the interval between the two : if the G.M.T. of birth is before the noon, then take the interval between the preceding noon and G.M.T. of birth. The result is Greenwich Mean Time interval of birth.

Nirayana Longitudes of Planets

Example 30.—*Find the G.M.T. interval of birth in the Standard Horoscope.*

The G.M.T. of Birth = 8–56 a.m.

∴ Take preceding noon (noon of 15-10-1918)

∴ G.M.T. interval of birth is 20h. 56m.

100. Daily Motions of Planets

The celestial arc traversed by the planets in a day is their daily motion. Take the arc that each planet has traversed from the noon preceding birth to the noon succeeding birth.

Example 31.—*Find the daily motions of planets in the Standard Horoscope.*

Referring to German Ephemeris for 1918, we get the following information :—

Planets	Long. on 16th Oct. at Noon	Long. on 15th Oct. at Noon	Daily Motions of the Planets
Sun (Libra)	22° 18′ 55″	21° 19′ 25″	0° 59′ 30″
Moon (Pisces)	4 24 0	20 5 0 (Aquarius)	14 19 0
Mars (Sagittarius)	10 50 0	10 7 0	0 43 0
Mercury (Libra)	23 1 0	21 19 0	1 42 0
Jupiter (Cancer)	15 18 0	15 14 0	0 4 0
Venus (Libra)	12 36 0	11 21 0	1 15 0
Saturn (Leo)	25 40 0	25 35 0	0 5 0
Rahu, Moon's ascending node (Sagit.)	15 46 0	15 43 0	0 3 0

101. Hindu Nirayana Longitudes of Planets

We know the daily movements of all the planets *i.e.*, the arc they pass through in 24 hours. Now find by proportion or with the aid of Logarithmic tables, the arc covered by each of them in the G.M.T. interval of birth and add this to their respective longitudes at the noon previous to birth. The result would represent their exact Sayana positions at the birth moment. If a planet is retrograde subtract the arc traversed in a day from its previous longitude. In case of Rahu, the arc must always be subtracted. In the case of the Sun and the Moon the arc must be always added. In the case of the other five planets the arc is additive or subtractive according as the planet is direct or retrograde. From the Sayana Longitudes so obtained, subtract Ayanamsa for the year of birth (see Art. 50) and the Hindu Nirayana Longitudes of the planets are obtained.

Rule 1.—Arc traversed in G.M.T. interval of birth.

$$= \frac{\text{Daily motion of the planet}}{24 \text{ hours}} \times \text{G.M.T. interval of birth.}$$

Rule 2.—Sayana Long. at birth =
  (a) Long. of planet at noon previous to birth $\pm$ arc traversed in G.M.T. interval of birth.
  + in case of Sun, Moon and other planets having direct motion, except Rahu.
  — in case of Retrograde planets and Rahu.
  (b) Rahu's Long. + 180° = Ketu's Long.

Rule 3.—Hindu Nirayana Long. = Sayana Long.—Ayanamsa.

Example 32.—*Find the Hindu Nirayana Longitudes of planets in the Standard Horoscope.*

G.M.T. interval of birth = 20h. 56m.

∴ arc traversed by each planet in 20h. 56m. +

Sun $\quad \dfrac{59' \ 30'' \times 20\text{h. } 56\text{m.}}{24} = 0° \ 51' \ 53''$

Nirayana Longitudes of Planets

$$\text{Mars} \quad \frac{0°\ 43' \times 20h.\ 56m.}{24} = 0°\ 40'\ 15''$$

$$\text{Mercury} \quad \frac{1°\ 42' \times 20h.\ 56m.}{24} = 1°\ 29'\ 15''$$

$$\text{Jupiter} \quad \frac{0°\ 4' \times 20h.\ 56m.}{24} = 0°\ 3'\ 30''$$

$$\text{Venus} \quad \frac{1°\ 15' \times 20h.\ 56m.}{24} = 1°\ 5'\ 37''$$

$$\text{Saturn} \quad \frac{0°\ 5' \times 20h.\ 56m.}{24} = 0°\ 4'\ 22''$$

$$\text{Rahu} \quad \frac{0°\ 3' \times 20h.\ 56m.}{24} = 0°\ 2'\ 32''$$

It is better to ascertain the arc traversed by the Moon by recourse to Logarithmic tables given at the end of the Ephemeris. If the reader cannot do this he can simply find the arc, as usual, by the rule of three,

Moon's daily motion	= 14° 19'
G.M.T. interval of birth	= 20h. 56m.
∴ Log 14° 19'	= 0.2244
∴ Log 20h. 56m.	= 0.0594
By adding	0.2838

∴ Anti Log of 0.2838 = 12° 29'

∴ Moon's motion in 20h. 56m. − 12° 29'.

Applying Rule 2 (*a* and *b*) we get their Sayana Longitudes thus :—

	Planets	Long. on 15th Oct.	Arc. covered in 20h. 56m.	Sayana Long. at Birth
1.	Sun	.... 201° 19' 25"	+ 0° 51' 11"	= 202° 10' 36"
2.	Moon	.... 320 5 0	+ 12 29 0	= 332 34 0
3.	Mars	.... 250 7 0	+ 0 40 15	= 250 47 15

Planets	Long. on 15th Oct.	Arc. covered in 20h. 56m.	Sayana Long. at Birth
4. Mercury	201° 19′ 0″	+ 1° 29′ 15″	= 202° 48′ 15″
5. Jupiter	105 14 0	+ 0 3 30	= 105 17 30
6. Venus	191 21 0	+ 1 5 37	= 192 26 37
7. Saturn	145 35 0	+ 0 4 22	= 145 39 22
8. Rahu	255 43 0	− 0 2 32	= 255 40 28
9. Ketu	....	....	= 75 40 28

Applying Rule 3 :—

Planets	Sayana Long. of planet at birth	Ayanamsa	Its Nirayana Long.
1. Sun	202° 10′ 36″	− 21° 16′ 41″	= 180° 53′ 55″
2. Moon	332 34 0	− 21 16 41	= 311 17 19
3. Mars	250 47 15	− 21 16 47	= 229 30 34
4. Mercury	202 48 15	− 21 16 47	= 181 31 34
5. Jupiter	105 17 30	− 21 16 41	= 84 0 49
6. Venus	192 26 37	− 21 16 41	= 171 9 56
7. Saturn	145 39 22	− 22 16 41	= 124 22 41
8. Rahu	255 40 28	− 21 16 41	= 234 23 47
9. Ketu	75 40 28	− 21 16 41	= 54 23 47

Now we have obtained the positions of grahas; we shall proceed to find out the different Bhavas.

102. The Sidereal Time of Birth

This is very essential for finding out the ascendant and other houses. You will see the Sidereal Time marked for G.M.N. every day in the first column of the Ephemeris, *i.e.*, next to weekday column. The Sidereal Time for birth must be obtained as follows :—

The Sidereal Time of Birth

First ascertain the Sidereal Time at the previous Greenwich Mean Noon. From or to this deduct or add at the rate of 10 seconds for every one hour of longitude, this being the correction for the difference of time between place of birth and Greenwich. Deduct if the place of birth is east of Greenwich, add if it is west of Greenwich. The Sidereal Time for the previous Local Mean Noon is obtained. Now add to this Mean Time interval (*i.e.*, the number of hours passed from previous local noon to birth) and also add 10 seconds per hour since noon, as this represents the difference between the Sidereal Time and the Mean Time. Expunge multiples of 24 hours. The result represents the Sidereal Time at birth.

Example 33.—*Find the Sidereal Time at Birth in the Standard Horoscope.*

L.M.T. of Birth = 2h. 6m. 16s. (P.M.)
Long. of Birth 77° 34' E = 5h. 10m. 16s.

	H.	M.	S.
Sidereal Time at G.M.N. of 16th Oct.	13	36	46
Less Correction for the difference of Time between the place of birth (East of Greenwich) and Greenwich ... −	0	0	52
∴ Sidereal Time at Local Noon ...	13	35	54
Add Number of hours passed from noon to birth (*i.e.*, Mean Time interval)	2	6	16
Add Correction between Sidereal Time and Mean Time at 10s. per hour	0	0	21
∴ Sidereal Time at Birth	15	42	31

103. R.A.M.C. at Birth

Convert Sidereal Time into arc. The result represents the R.A.M.C. at birth, *i.e.*, Sidereal Time × 15° = R.A.M.C. at birth.

Example 34.—*Find the R.A.M.C. for the given Sidereal Time at birth as 15h. 42m. 31s. in the Standard Horoscope.*

15h.	=	225° 0' 0"
42m.	=	10 30 0
31s.	=	0 8 0
∴ R.A.M.C. at birth	=	235° 38' 0"

104. Sayana Longitudes of Angular Houses

Since there is a slight difference between the Hindu and western methods of computing the longitudes of the non-angular houses, we shall ascertain those of the angular houses from the Modern Table of Houses, reduce them into Nirayana ones and then find out the longitudes of the non-angular houses according to the rules described in Article 88.

Consider the "Table of Houses" for the latitude of the birthplace; if no Table of Houses for the birthplace is available, then refer to that which is nearest to the latitude of birth. Find the nearest time corresponding to Local Sidereal Time of Birth (under the column Sidereal Time). Next to that we see the cusp of the tenth house; mark its longitude; trace further and you will see a column marked as "Ascendant"; mark its longitude also. Deduct from these two, the Ayanamsa. Their Nirayana Bhava Madhyas are

Sayana Longitudes

obtained, *i.e.*, the longitudes of Udaya Lagna (Ascendant) and the Upper Meridian (Madhya Lagna) are obtained. Adding 180° to each of these two, the Nirayana Asta Lagna (Western Horizon) and the Pathala Lagna (Lower Meridian) are obtained. Now apply the rules contained in Articles 87, 88, 89, 90 and 91. Now you have the horoscope ready.

Example 35.—*Find the Sayana Longitudes of the cusps of the ascendant and the 10th house in the Standard Horoscope and reduce them to those of Nirayana.*

Sidereal Time at Birth = 15h. 42m. 30s.
Birthplace, 13° North Latitude.
∴ The Table of Houses for the birth latitude must be consulted.
15h. 42m. 30s. is the Sidereal Time of Birth.
∴ Sayana Long. of cusp of ascdt. = 19° 48′ 41″ Aquarius
∴ Sayana Long. of cusp of tenth house = 27° 52′ 41″
          Scorpio or 237° 52′ 41″

Sayana Long. of the cusp of the house	Ayanamsa	Nirayana Long. of Bhava Madhya
Ascdt. 319° 43′ 51″	— 21° 16′ 41″	= 298° 41′
10th House : 237° 52′ 41″	— 21° 16′ 41″	= 216° 36′

∴ Asta Lagna (W. Horizon) = 298° — 27′ + 180° = 118° 27′
 Pathala Lagna (Lower Meridian) = 216° — 36 + 180°
               = 36° 36′.

Applying the rules described in Articles 87, 81, 89, 91 and 96, the Longitudes of Bhava Madhyas of the Non-angular Houses, Bhava-Sandhis, Poorva and Uttara Bhagas of the Bhavas and the length of each Bhava can be determined: For these details refer to examples 27 and 28 of Chapter X (Pp. 109 and 110).

105. Nirayana Tables

The need for deducting Ayanamsa and calculating the longitudes of the houses by first determining the rising sign (Udaya Lagna) and the tenth house (Madhya Lagna) can be dispensed with by the use of *The Nirayana Tables of Houses*. The sphutas (longitudes) for the ascendant and the 10th, 11th and 12th houses are given and the sphutas for other houses can be easily obtained by simple calculations. These Tables have this additional advantage, *viz.*, that they are calculated for the Ayanamsa adopted by the author, and cover all places between the equator and 60° Latitude.

	Ketu	Jupit.			Ketu	Jupiter
Moon	RASI KUNDALI			BHAVA KUNDALI		Saturn
Ascdt.		Sat.	Ascdt. Moon			
	Mars Rahu	Sun Merc.	Venus		Mars Rahu	Venus Sun Merc

CHAPTER XII

The Shodasavargas

106. The Vargas

The Zodiac or the Bhachakra is composed of 360 degrees of the celestial space. 30 degrees constitute one sign of the zodiac. Each of these signs is further subdivided into a number of other divisions, *i.e.*, into certain kinds of divisions. These kinds of divisions are known as the Vargas. These are based on the assumption that planets increase or decrease in their capacity to produce good or inflict bad, in a horoscope, according to their particular positions within a sign. They become highly potent by occupying certain kinds of divisions, owned by them, or by planets declared as their intimate friends, or by such divisions being their own places of exaltation or fall. These various relations like elevation (Uchcha), fall (Neecha), etc., have been already discussed elsewhere*.

For predictive purposes the varga or division charts can be used with great advantage—*e.g.*, Rasi —body, general strength of the chart; Hora— wealth; Drekkana—brothers and sisters; Chaturthamsa—education; Saptamsa—children; Navamsa

---
* For further information see my book *Graha and Bhava Balas*.

—husband or wife; Dasamsa—occupation; Dwadasamsa—parents; Shodasamsa—cherished desires; Vimsamsa—scientific and spiritual achievements; Chaturvimsamsa—academic attainments; Bhamsa—misfortunes; Khavedamsa—good and bad; Thrimsamsa, Akshavedamsa and Shashtyamsa.

107. The Varga Divisions

They are really sixteen in number. But the number adopted by different astrologers varies according to how they are used. For instance, for finding out the *Sthanabala* (positional strength) of a planet, the Saptavargas are considered. For making predictions, the Shadvargas are employed. Some consider Dasavargas and so on, the choice often depending upon the prevailing custom. We shall, for purposes of determining the Sthanabala of planets, go in detail into Saptavargas and scan through all the sixteen vargas rather superficially.

108. The Shadvargas

They are (1) Rasi, (2) Hora, (3) Drekkana, (4) Navamsa, (5) Dwadasamsa and (6) Thrimsamsa.

109. The Saptavargas

(1) Rasi, (2) Hora, (3) Drekkana, (4) Sapthamsa, (5) Navamsa, (6) Dwadasamsa and (7) Thrimsamsa.

110. The Dasavargas

(1) Rasi, (2) Hora, (3) Drekkana, (4) Sapthamsa, (5) Navamsa, (6) Dasamsa, (7) Dwadasamsa,

Rasi 123

(8) Shodasamsa, (9) Thrimsamsa and (10) Shashtyamsa.

111. The Shodasa Vargas

(1) Rasi, (2) Hora, (3) Drekkana, (4) Chaturthamsa, (5) Sapthamsa, (6) Navamsa, (7) Dasamsa, (8) Dwadasamsa, (9) Shodasamsa, (10) Vimsamsa, (11) Chathurvimsamsa, (12) Bhamsa, (13) Thrimsamsa, (14) Khavedamsa, (15) Aksha Vedamsa and (16) Shashtyamsa.

We shall now describe the various vargas, and the methods of locating the planets in each one of them.

112. Rasi

Rasi means sign. The 12 signs of the zodiac are the 12 Rasis. The limits and the lordships of the various Rasis are named in the second chapter. The Rasivarga is employed for predicting events pertaining to the body.

Example 36.—*Find the Rasis of the different planets and the Lagna in the Standard Horoscope and the lords of such Rasis.*

Planet	Its Long.	Rasi	Lord of the Rasi
Ravi	180° 53' 55"	Thula	Sukra
Chandra	311 17 19	Kumbha	Sani
Kuja	229 30 34	Vrischika	Kuja
Budha	181 31 34	Thula	Sukra
Guru	84 0 49	Mithuna	Budha
Sukra	171 9 56	Kanya	Budha
Sani	124 22 41	Simha	Ravi
Rahu	234 23 47	Vrischika	Kuja
Ketu	54 23 47	Vrishabha	Sukra
Lagna	298 27 0	Makara	Sani

113. Hora

2½ ghatis constitute 1 hora; 15 degrees are equal to one hour in time so that, on the whole, there are 24 hours of 15° each in the entire zodiac. Each sign contains 2 horas, namely, the Surya Hora (Sun's) and the Chandra Hora (Moon's). In Oja Rasis or odd signs the first hora is governed by the Sun and the second by the Moon. In Yugma Rasis or even signs the ruler of the first hora is the Moon, and second hora is governed by the Sun. Odd signs are Mesha, Mithuna, Simha, etc. Even signs are Vrishabha, Kataka, Kanya, etc. For instance, the first hora in Mesha is governed by the Sun, while the second is presided over by the Moon. Similarly so with reference to Mithuna, etc. In Vrishabha, Chandra presides over the first hora and the Sun over the next. The 'Hora' chart is employed for studying wealth.

Example 37.—*Find the Horas occupied by the planets, and the lords of such Horas in the Standard Horoscope.*

Planet	Its Long.	Nature of Rasi	Hora	Its Lord
Ravi	180° 53' 55"	Oja	Surya	Surya
Chandra	311 17 19	Oja	Surya	Surya
Kuja	229 30 34	Yugma	Surya	Surya
Budha	181 31 34	Oja	Surya	Surya
Guru	84 0 49	Oja	Chandra	Chandra
Sukra	171 9 56	Yugma	Surya	Surya
Sani	124 22 41	Oja	Surya	Surya
Lagna	298 27 0	Yugma	Surya	Surya

Drekkana 125

We shall omit Rahu and Ketu for the present, as they are considered Aprakashaka Grahas or shadowy planets and as they simply reflect the results of the lords of the houses they occupy.

114. Drekkana

The zodiac is divided into 36 Drekkanas so that each gets 10°. The lord of the first Drekkana in a Rasi is the lord of the Rasi itself; that of the second, the lord of the 5th from it; that of the 3rd, the lord of the 9th from it.

Rasi	Lord of its 1st Drekkana	Lord of its 2nd Drekkana	Lord of its 3rd Drekkana
Mesha	Kuja	Ravi	Guru
Vrishabha	Sukra	Budha	Sani
Mithuna	Budha	Sukra	Sani
Kataka	Chandra	Kuja	Guru
Simha	Ravi	Guru	Kuja
Kanya	Budha	Sani	Sukra
Thula	Sukra	Sani	Budha
Vrischika	Kuja	Guru	Chandra
Dhanus	Guru	Kuja	Ravi
Makara	Sani	Sukra	Budha
Kumbha	Sani	Budha	Sukra
Meena	Guru	Chandra	Kuja

Example 38.—*Find the various Drekkanas occupied by the planets and the lords of such Drekkanas in the Standard Horoscope.*

Planet	1st Long.	No. of Drekkana	Its Lord
Ravi	180° 53' 55"	1st in Thula	Sukra
Chandra	311 17 19	2nd in Kumbha	Budha
Kuja	229 30 34	2nd in Vrischika	Guru
Budha	181 31 34	1st in Thula	Sukra

Planet	Ist Long.			No. of Drekkana	Its Lord
Guru	84	0	49	3rd in Mithuna	Sani
Sukra	171	9	56	3rd in Kanya	Sukra
Sani	124	22	41	1st in Simha	Ravi
Lagna	298	27	0	3rd in Makara	Budha

115. Chaturthamsa

When a sign is divided into four equal parts, each one is called Chaturthamsa. The zodiac contains 48 Chaturthamsas and each is equal to $\frac{360}{48}$ or 7° 30' of the celestial space. The lord of the 1st Chaturthamsa is the lord of the Rasi itself; that of the 2nd, the lord of the 4th from it; that of the 3rd, the lord of the 7th and that of the 4th, the lord of the 10th. Thus the lord of each Kendra Rasi (quadrant) becomes the lord of each Chaturthamsa.

Example 39.—*Find the Chaturthamsa the planets and the Lagna have occupied and the lords of such Chaturthamsas in the Standard Horoscope.*

Planet	Its Long.			No. of the Chaturthamsa	Lord of Chaturthamsa
Ravi	180°	153'	55"	1st —	Sukra
Chandra	311	17	19	2nd —	,,
Kuja	229	30	34	3rd —	,,
Budha	181	31	34	1st —	,,
Guru	84	0	49	4th —	Guru
Sukra	171	9	56	3rd —	Guru
Sani	124	22	41	1st —	Ravi
Lagna	298	27	0	4th —	Sukra

116. Sapthamsa

When a sign is divided into seven equal divisions, each is called a Sapthamsa and gets $\frac{30}{7} = 4° 17' 8\frac{4}{7}''$. The Bhachakra is divided into 84 Sapthamsas. In odd signs they are governed by the lords of the first seven Rasis and in even signs by the lords of the seventh and following signs.

Example 40.—*Find the Sapthamsa the planets and the Lagna have occupied, and the lords of Such Sapthamsas in the Standard Horoscope.*

Planet	Its Long.	Odd or Even Rasi	No. of the Sapthamsa	Lord of Sapthamsa
Ravi ...	180° 53' 55"	Odd	1st	Sukra
Chandra	311 17 19	Odd	3rd	Kuja
Kuja ...	229 30 34	Even	5th	Budha
Budha ...	181 31 34	Odd	1st	Sukra
Guru ...	84 0 49	Odd	6th	Kuja
Sukra ...	171 9 56	Even	5th	Chandra
Sani ...	124 22 41	Odd	2nd	Budha
Lagna ...	298 27 0	Even	7th	Sani

117. Navamsa

This is the most important subdivision among the Hindus. The successful forecasts made by them have this system as the basis. This has been formulated in view of the relationship between the degrees of the ecliptic and the stellar points of nakshatras. The nakshatras are 27 in number (Art. 10). Therefore each nakshatra gets $13\frac{1}{3}$ degrees. Each nakshatra is further subdivided into padas or quarters, so that one pada is equal to $\frac{13\frac{1}{3}°}{4} = 3\frac{1}{3}°$ of the ecliptic arc.

Similarly a sign is divided into nine equal parts and each is a navamsa. The Bhachakra is divided into 108 navamsas and each navamsa corresponds to a *Nakshatra Pada*. Reference to the schedule of nakshatras given in Art. 10 will tell you that 4 quarters of Aswini, 4 of Bharani, and one of Krittika make up Mesha. By knowing the nakshatra padas of Grahas we can readily locate them in their precise Navamsa Vargas.

Take Mesha and divide it into nine equal parts. The first part (Navamsa) is governed by the lord of Mesha, *viz.*, Kuja; the second by the lord of the second, *viz.*, Sukra; the third by Budha the lord of the third; the fourth by the lord of the fourth, *viz.*, Chandra, and so on till the last or the ninth navamsa which is governed by Jupiter, lord of the ninth from Mesha. Now divide Vrishabha into nine equal parts. We have left counting of the navamsa at Dhanus, *viz.*, the ninth from Mesha. Therefore, the first navamsa of Taurus (or the 10th navamsa from Mesha) is governed by the lord of the 10th from Mesha, *viz.*, lord of Makara—Sani; the second navamsa (in Vrishabha), by the lord of the 11th from Mesha, *viz.*, Sani; the 3rd by the lord of the 12th, *viz.*, Guru; the 4th, 5th, 6th, 7th, 8th and 9th by Kuja, Sukra, Budha, Chandra, Ravi and Budha respectively. Then the first navamsa of Mithuna is ruled by the lord of the 7th from Aries, *viz.*, Sukra. The last navamsa of Gemini is governed by the lord of the

Navamsa

ninth from Libra, *viz.*, Mercury. Again the first of Cancer is governed by the lord of Cancer and the last navamsa of Cancer by the lord of ninth from Cancer, *viz.*, Jupiter, so that, the first navamsa in Leo is ruled by the lord of tenth from Cancer-Aries, *viz.*, Mars. It invariably follows, that for Mesha, Simha and Dhanus navamsas must be counted from Mesha to Dhanus; for Vrishabha, Kanya and Makara from Makara; for Mithuna, Thula and Kumbha from Thula; and for Kataka, Vrischika and Meena from Kataka. Thus we see four distinct groups given.

(a) Mesha, Simha, Dhanus — from Mesha.
(b) Vrishabha, Kanya, Makara — from Makara.
(c) Mithuna, Thula, Kumbha — from Thula.
(d) Kataka, Vrischika, Meena — from Kataka.

Take for instance a planet whose longitude is $114° 26' 15''$ or $24° 26' 15''$ in Cancer. Note this belongs to group (d) so that the navamsas must be counted from Kataka. $24° 26' 15'' \div 3\frac{1}{3} = 7$ and odd navamsas. The planet has passed 7 navamsas in Cancer and is in the 8th. The 8th navamsa in Cancer is ruled by the lord of the 8th Rasi from Cancer, *viz.*, Aquarius—Saturn. Thus the planet is in Saturn's navamsa.

In group (a) the lords of the nine navamsas will be the lords of Mesha and the succeeding signs. Similarly with reference to other groups, the navamsas must be considered.

Example 4.— *Find the Navamsa occupied by the planets and the Lagna, and the lords of such Navamsas in the Standard Horoscope.**

Planet	Its Long.	No. of the Navamsa	Its Lord
Ravi	180° 53' 55"	1st in Thula	Sukra
Chandra	311 17 19	4th in Kumbha	Sani
Kuja	229 30 34	6th in Vrischika	Guru
Budha	181 31 34	1st in Thula	Sukra
Guru	84 0 49	8th in Mithuna	Sukra
Sukra	171 9 56	7th in Kanya	Chandra
Sani	124 22 41	2nd in Simha	Sukra
Lagna	298 27 0	9th in Makara	Budha
Rahu	234 23 47	8th in Vrischika	Sani
Ketu	54 23 47	8th in Vrishabha	Ravi

118. Navamsas and Nakshatra Padas

Now that we have learnt how to find in which navamsa a planet is situated, we can also easily find out the particular constellation and the particular pada the planet is in. For instance, take the Sun. He occupies the 1st navamsa in Thula, *i.e.*, he is in the 1st pada of Thula Rasi. The schedule of constellations in Chapter II will tell you that the last two padas of Chitta, four padas of Swathi and the three padas of Visakha make up Thula. Note to which pada (quarter) and nakshatra (constellation) in Thula, the 1st navamsa corresponds.

Thula	Chitta	2	Padas
	Swathi	4	,,
	Visakha	3	,,

---
* Include Rahu and Ketu also.

Therefore, the 1st navamsa of Thula corresponds to the third of Chitta. Therefore you say that the Sun is in the third pada (quarter) of the nakshatra (constellation) Chitta. Ascertain for all the planets, the nakshatras and the padas corresponding to the navamsa positions.

Example 42.—*Find the Nakshatra Pada occupied by the different planets and the Lagna (of course Bhava Madhya) in the Standard Horoscope.*

Planet	Rasi	No. of Navamsa	Nakshtra	Pada
Ravi	Thula	1st	Chitta	3
Chandra	Kumbha	4th	Satabhisha	2
Kuja	Vrischika	6th	Jyeshta	1
Budha	Thula	1st	Chitta	3
Guru	Mithuna	8th	Punarvasu	2
Sukra	Kanya	7th	Hastha	4
Sani	Simha	2nd	Makha	2
Lagna	Makara	9th	Dhanishta	2
Rahu	Vrischika	8th	Jyeshta	3
Ketu	Vrishabha	8th	Mrigasira	1

119. Navamsa Chakra

As navamsa combinations are referred to very often in *Hindu Predictive Astrology* it would be better to mark the Grahas in a navamsa diagram for purposes of convenience and reference.

Example 43.—*Locate the planets and Lagna of the Standard Horoscope in a Navamsa Kundali.*

		♉ Guru Sani	♊
♓			
♒ Rahu	NAVAMSA DIAGRAM		♋ Sukra
♑ Chandra			♌ Ketu
♐ Kuja	♍	♎ Ravi Budha	♏ Lagna

120. The Dasamsa

When a sign is divided into ten equal parts, each is called a Dasamsa, meaning $\frac{1}{10}$th of it. The whole Zodiac gets 120 Dasamsas of 3° each.

In odd signs the lord of the Dasamsas commence from the owner of the sign itself, while in even signs the rulers are the lords of the ninth* and the following house respectively.

Example 44.—*Find the Dasamsa the planets and the Lagna have occupied and the lords of such Dasamsa in the Standard Horoscope.*

Planet	Its Long.			No. of Dasamsa	Lord of Dasamsa
Ravi	180°	53′	55″	1st	Sukra
Chandra	311	17	19	4th	Sukra
Kuja	229	30	34	7th	Sani

---

* *See Sarvartha Chintamani*, English translation by Prof. B. Suryanarain Rao, Stanza 21, Chapter I.

Planet	Its Long.			No. of Dasamsa	Lord of Dasamsa
Budha	181	31	34	1st	Sukra
Guru	84	0	49	9th	Sani
Sukra	171	9	56	8th	Guru
Sani	124	22	41	2nd	Budha
Lagna	298	27	0	10th	Budha

121. Dwadasamsa

When a sign is divided into 12 equal parts, each is called a Dwadasamsa and measures $2\frac{1}{2}°$. The Bhachakra can thus be said to contain $12 \times 12 = 144$ Dwadasamsas. The lords of the Dwadasamsas in a sign are lords of the 12 signs from it, *i.e.*, the lord of the first Dwadasamsa in Mesha is Kuja, that of the second Sukra and so on.

Example 45.—*Find the Dwadasamsa occupied by the various planets and the Lagna in the Standard Horoscope and the lords of such Dwadasamsas.*

Planet	Its Long.			No. of Dwadasamsa	Lord of Dwadasamsa
Ravi	180°	53'	55"	1st in Thula	Sukra
Chandra	311	17	19	5th in Kumbha	Budha
Kuja	229	30	34	8th in Vrischika	Budha
Budha	181	31	34	1st in Thula	Sukra
Guru	84	0	49	10th in Mithuna	Guru
Sukra	171	9	56	9th in Kanya	Sukra
Sani	124	22	41	2nd in Simha	Budha
Lagna	298	27	0	12th in Makara	Guru

122. Shodasamsa

When a sign is divided into 16 equal parts, each is called a Shodasamsa. The Bhachakra contains

16 × 12 = 192 Shodasamsas. The lords of the sixteen Shodasamsas in movable, fixed and common signs are the lords of the signs counted from Aries, Leo and Sagittarius respectively. Thus in Aries (a movable sign) the sixteen lords are Mars, Venus, Mercury, Moon, Sun, Mercury, Venus, Mars, Jupiter, Saturn, Saturn, Jupiter, Mars, Venus, Mercury and Moon. Take for example Aquarius. It is a fixed sign. The count starts from Leo and the lords of the 16 Shodasamsas will respectively be Sun, Mercury, Venus, Mars, Jupiter, Saturn, Saturn, Jupiter, Mars, Venus, Mercury, Moon, Sun, Mercury, Venus and Mars.

The counting is always clockwise.

Example 46.—*Find the Shodasamsa occupied by the various planets and the Lagna in the Standard Horoscope and lord of such Shodasamsa.*

Planet	Its Long.	No. of Shodasamsa	Lord of Shodasamsa
Ravi	180° 53' 55"	1st	Kuja
Chandra	311 17 19	7th	Sani
Kuja	229 30 34	11th	Budha
Budha	181 31 34	1st	Kuja
Guru	84 0 49	13th	Guru
Sukra	171 9 56	12th	Kuja
Sani	124 22 41	3rd	Sukra
Lagna	298 27 0	16th	Chandra

123. Vimsamsa

When a sign is divided into twenty parts, each is called a Vimsamsa, the length of the arc being

Chaturvimsamsa

1° 30'. The twenty Vimsamsas in a movable, fixed and common signs are ruled by the lords of signs counted from Aries, Sagittarius and Leo respectively. Thus in Aries (which is movable) the lords of the Vimsamsas are Mars, Venus, Mercury, Moon, Sun, Mercury, Venus, Mars, Jupiter, Saturn, Saturn, Jupiter, Mars, Venus, Mercury, Moon, Sun, Mercury, Venus, and Mars. In Taurus for instance, the ruler of the first Vimsamsa is Jupiter, lord of Sagittarius and the other lords follow in regular order. In Gemini, the lord of the first Vimsamsa is the Sun, lord of Leo and the other parts are governed by Mercury, Venus, etc., counted clockwise.

Example 47.—*Find the Vimsamsa occupied by various planets and the Lagna in the Standard Horoscope and the lord of such Vimsamsas*

Planet	Its Long.	No. of Vimsamsa	Lord of Vimsamsa
Ravi	180° 53' 55"	1st	Kuja
Chandra	311 17 19	8th	Chandra
Kuja	229 30 34	14th	Sani
Budha	181 31 34	2nd	Sukra
Guru	84 0 49	17th	Guru
Sukra	171 9 56	15th	Sukra
Sani	124 22 41	3rd	Sani
Lagna	298 27 0	19th	Sukra

124. Chaturvimsamsa

Each one-twenty-fourth part of a sign goes under the name of *Chaturvimsamsa*. There are 24 × 12 = 288 Vimsamsas in the zodiac. In odd signs, the lord of the first division is the Sun. Lords of subsequent divisions follow in order. In even signs, the lord of the 1st part is the Moon and the 2nd, 3rd, etc., lordships go to the Sun, Mercury, Venus, etc., in regular order. The count is always clockwise.

Example 48.—*Find the Chaturvimsamsa occupied by the various planets and the Lagna in the Standard Horoscope and the lord of such Chaturvimsamsa.*

Planet	Its Long.	No. of Chatur-vimsamsa	Lord of Chatur-vimsamsa
Ravi	180° 53' 55"	1st	Ravi
Chandra	311 17 19	10th	Sukra
Kuja	229 30 34	16th	Sukra
Budha	181 31 34	2nd	Budha
Guru	84 0 49	20th	Guru
Sukra	171 9 56	17th	Kuja
Sani	124 22 41	4th	Kuja
Lagna	298 27 0	23rd	Sukra

125. Bhamsa

When a sign is divided into 27 parts, each part is called a Bhamsa. Thus there are in the entire zodiac 27 × 12 = 324 Bhamsas. (*a*) In Aries, Leo and Sagittarius, the 27 parts are governed by the lords of the signs counted in regular order from Aries. (*b*) In Taurus, Virgo and Capricorn, the rulership begins from Cancer. (*c*) In Gemini, Libra and Aquarius, the counting starts from Libra. (*d*) In Cancer, Scorpio and Pisces, the Bhamsas are governed by the lords of signs reckoned from Capricorn. For example take

Virgo. It falls in group (b). Therefore the count must start from Cancer. The lord of the 1st Bhamsa in Virgo is the lord of Cancer, *viz.*, Moon. The other lords will be the Sun, Mercury, Venus, Mars, Jupiter, Saturn, Saturn, Jupiter, Mars, Venus, Mercury, Moon, Sun, Mercury, Venus, Mars, Jupiter, Saturn, Saturn, Jupiter, Mars, Venus, Mercury, Moon, Sun and Mercury respectively.

Example 49.—*Find the Bhamsa occupied by the various planets and the Lagna in the Standard Horoscope and the lord of such Bhamsas.*

Planet	Its Long.	No. of Bhamsa	Lord of Bhamsa
Ravi	180° 53' 55"	1st	Sukra
Chandra	311 17 19	11th	Ravi
Kuja	229 30 34	18th	Budha
Budha	181 31 34	2nd	Kuja
Guru	84 0 49	22nd	Chandra
Sukra	171 9 56	20th	Sani
Sani	124 22 41	4th	Chandra
Lagna	298 27 0	26th	Ravi

126. Thrimsamsa

When a sign is divided into 30 equal parts, each is called a Thrimsamsa measuring 1° each. In odd signs, the Thrimsamsas are governed thus :—

Mars	Saturn	Jupiter	Mercury	Venus
5	5	8	7	5 = 30

In even signs the order must be reversed :—

Venus	Mercury	Jupiter	Saturn	Mars
5	7	8	5	5 = 30

The above may be interpreted thus :—

In Mesha, Mithuna and such other Oja (odd) Rasis, the first 5 Thrimsamsas are governed by Mars, the second 5 by Saturn and so on. In Yugma Rasis (even signs) like Vrishabha, Kataka, etc., the first 5 are governed by Venus, the next 5 by Mercury, etc., as mentioned above.

Example 50.—*Find the number of the Thrimsamsas occupied by the planets and the Lagna in the Standard Horoscope and the lords of such Thrimsamsas.*

Planet	Its Long.	No. of Thrimsamsa	Lord of Thrimsamsa
Ravi	180° 53′ 55″	1st in odd	Kuja
Chandra	311 17 19	12th in odd	Guru
Kuja	229 30 34	20th in even	Guru
Budha	181 31 34	2nd in odd	Kuja
Guru	84 0 49	25th in odd	Budha
Sukra	171 9 56	22nd in even	Sani
Sani	124 22 41	5th in odd	Kuja
Lagna	298 27 0	29th in even	Kuja

127. Khavedamsa

When a sign is divided into 40 equal parts, each part goes under the name of Khavedamsa, measuring 0° 45′ of arc. There are 480 such divisions in the entire zodiac. In odd signs, the lords of the 40 Khavedamsas are the rulers of the signs counted from Aries onwards, in a regular order, repeating the counting. In even signs the lords are the owners of the signs, counted from Libra in a regular order. Thus in Aries, the lord of the 1st division will be Mars, 13th Mars, 25th Mars, 37th Mars and the 40th Moon.

In Cancer, an even sign, the lord of the 1st division is Venus (lord of Libra), 13th Venus, 25th Venus, 37th Venus and 40th Saturn. The reckoning is simple and needs no elaboration.

Example 51.—*Find the number of the Khavedamsa occupied by the planets and the Lagna in the Standard Horoscope and the lords of such Khavedamsas.*

Planet	Its Long.	No. of Khavedamsa	Its Lord
Ravi	180° 53' 55"	2nd in odd sign	Sukra
Chandra	311 17 19	16th in odd sign	Chandra
Kuja	229 30 34	27th in even sign	Guru
Budha	181 31 34	3rd in odd sign	Budha
Guru	84 0 49	33rd in add sign	Guru
Sukra	171 9 56	29th in even sign	Sani
Sani	124 22 41	6th in odd sign	Budha
Lagna	298 27 0	38th in even sign	Kuja

128. Akshavedamsa

When a sign is divided into 45 parts, each part measuring 0° 40' goes under the name of Akshavedamsa. The 45 parts are governed by the lords of the signs counted regularly from Aries, Leo or Sagittarius according as the sign concerned is movable, fixed or common. Thus in Aries, Kuja will be the lord of 1st, 13th, 25th, 37th Akshavedamsa as Aries recurs three times. In Taurus, Ravi will be the lord of the 1st, 13th, 25th and 37th parts. In Gemini, Guru will be the lord of the 1st, 13th, 25th and 37th parts.

Example 52.—*Find the lords of Akshavedamsa occupied by planets and the Lagna in the Standard Horoscope and the lords of such Akshavedamsas.*

Planet	Its Long.	No. of Akshavedamsa	Its Lord
Ravi	180° 53′ 55″	2nd in Thula	Sukra
Chandra	311 17 19	17th in Kumbha	Guru
Kuja	229 30 34	30th in Vrischika	Sani
Budha	181 31 34	3rd in Thula	Budha
Guru	84 0 49	36th in Mithuna	Kuja
Sukra	171 9 56	32nd in Kanya	Chandra
Sani	124 22 41	7th in Simha	Sani
Lagna	298 27 0	43rd in Makara	Sukra

129. Shashtyamsa

When a sign is divided into 60 equal parts, each is called a Shashtyamsa, the extent being 0° 30′. Usually in text-books, the planetary lord of a Shashtyamsa is not given but only the Deity governing the amsa. For the information of readers, we shall give both in this article.

Rejecting the sign multiply the longitude of a planet by 2. Divide the product by 12. The remainder *plus* 1, counted from the sign position of the planet, represents the Shashtyamsa Rasi, the ruler of which is the Shashtyamsa lord. The product *plus* 1 (counted in regular or reverse order according as the sign occupied by the planet is odd or even) denotes the particular Shashtyamsa according to the table given below.

In case of odd signs, the 60 Shashtyamsas are:—
(1) Ghora, (2) Rakhsasa, (3) Devabhaga, (4) Kubera, (5) Rakshogana, (6) Kinnara, (7) Hrusta, (8) Kalagnana, (9) Garala, (10) Aganighatha, (11) Mayamsa, (12) Preta Puriha, (13)

Apampathy, (14) Devaganasa, (15) Kala, (16) Sarpa, (17) Amritha, (18) Chandra, (19) Mridwamsa, (20) Komalamsa, (21) Padma, (22) Lakshmisa, (23) Vageesa, (24) Digambara, (25) Devamsa, (26) Indra, (27) Kalinasa, (28) Kshitiswara, (29) Kamalakara, (30) Mandatmaja, (31) Mrityu, (32) Kala, (33) Davagnya, (34) Ghora, (35) Yamakantaka, (36) Satya, (37) Amrita, (38) Paripurna, (39) Vishapradagdha, (40) Kulanasa, (41) Mukhya, (42) Vamsakshaya, (43) Ootpatha, (44) Kalarupa, (45) Soumya, (46) Mrudvamsa, (47) Susithala, (48) Damshtra, (49) Seethabja, (50) Indumukha, (51) Poorna, (52) Kalagnya, (53) Dandayudha, (54) Nirmala, (55) Shubha, (56) Ashubha, (57) Atishubha, (58) Sudhapayodhi, (59) Dhyumani, (60) Indurekha.

In case of even signs, the order of naming must be reversed.

Take for example Jupiter. He occupies 24° 01' of Gemini. Rejecting the sign and multiplying the longitude by 2 we get 48° 02' as product. Dividing this by 12, the remainder is 0°. The remainder *plus* one (0+1=1) counted from Gemini (the sign held by Jupiter) represents Cancer. Hence Jupiter's Shashtyamsa sign is Cancer and Shashtyamsa lord is Moon.

Now the product *plus* 1 (48+1=49) counted in direct order (Gemini is an odd sign) gives Seethabja.

130. Other Amsas

For the information of readers, we propose to give some more divisional reckonings which are employed by some astrologers for studying certain aspects of the horoscope. These divisions are not included by Parasara in what he calls the shodasamsas or 16 types of divisions. We shall briefly describe (1) Panchamsa, (2) Shashtamsa, (3) Ekadasamsa and (4) Nadi Amsa.

131. Panchamsa

Each Panchamsa—1/5th of a sign is 6° in extent, *i.e.*, the zodiac is divided into 60 Panchamsas. In odd signs the first Panchamsa is governed by Mars; the second by Saturn; the third by Jupiter; the fourth by Mercury; and the fifth by Venus. The reverse holds good in even signs.

132. Shashtamsa

There are 72 shashtamsas in the whole of the Bhachakra. Each shashtamsa is equal to five degrees and a Rasi is divided into 6 shashtamsas. In odd signs the lords of the six shashtamsas are the lords of the six houses from Aries and in even signs the lords of the six shashtamsas are the lords of the six Rasis from Libra.

133. Ashtamsa

An Ashtamsa measures 3° 45'. The Bhachakra is divided into 96 Ashtamsas and each Rasi, therefore, contains eight compartments—Ashtamsas. In movable signs (Aries, Cancer, etc.), the lords of the 8 Ashtamsas are the lords of the 8 signs from Aries. In Sthira Rasis or immovable signs (Taurus, Leo, etc.), the lords of the 8 Ashtamsas are those of Leo and succeeding signs. In Dwiswabhava Rasis (common signs like Gemini, Virgo, etc.), the 8 Ashtamsas are governed by the lords of Dhanus and the next 8 succeeding signs.

134. Ekadasamsa

Each Ekadasamsa measures $\frac{30°}{11} = 2° 43\frac{7}{11}$ or the Bhachakra contains 132 Ekadasamsas. The lords of the 11 Ekadasamsas are the lords of the eleven signs from the 12th Rasi, counted backwards. Thus in Aries the first Ekadasamsa is ruled by Jupiter, the lord of the 12th from it and so on.

135. Nadi Amsa

Each sign or Rasi is divided into 150 parts so that each part comes under the name of a Nadi Amsa measuring 12 minutes of arc. This minute division sets the seed of the destiny of an individual. If the correct Nadi Amsa is established, then there is a bird's eye view of the entire past and future of the person concerned. In fact Satyacharya says that in the absence of the correct Nadi Amsa, the time of birth cannot be decided accurately.

I give here the names of the 150 Nadi Amsas. They are :—

1 Vasudha	30 Kalusha	59 Preetha
2 Vaishnavi	31 Kamala	60 Priyavardhini
3 Brahmi	32 Kantha	61 Managni
4 Kalakuta	33 Kala	62 Durbhaga
5 Sankari	34 Karikara	63 Chitra
6 Sudhakari	35 Kshama	64 Chitrini
7 Sama	36 Durdhura	65 Chiranjivini
8 Soumya	37 Durbhaga	66 Bhoopa
9 Sura	38 Vishwa	67 Gadahari
10 Maya	39 Vishirna	68 Nala
11 Manohara	40 Vikala	69 Nalini
12 Madhvi	41 Vila	70 Nirmala
13 Manjuswana	42 Vibhrama	71 Nadi
14 Ghora	43 Sukhada	72 Sudha
15 Kumbhini	44 Snigda	73 Amrutamsa-kalika
16 Kutila	45 Sodari	
17 Prabha	46 Surasundari	74 Palakshan-kura
18 Para	47 Amritaplavini	
19 Payaswini	48 Kahala	75 Trailokya
20 Mala	49 Kamadruk	76 Mohanakari
21 Jagadhi	50 Kravirani	77 Mahaduti
22 Jarjhara	51 Gahana	78 Suseethala
23 Dhruva	52 Kuttini	79 Sukhada
24 Musala	53 Roudri	80 Suprabha
25 Mudgara	54 Vishakhya	81 Sobha
26 Pasa	55 Vishanasini	82 Subhada
27 Champaka	56 Narmada	83 Sobhana
28 Damini	57 Seetala	84 Sivada
29 Mahi	58 Nimna	85 Asiva

86 Bhala	108 Kumari	130 Shivakari
87 Jwala	109 Kokila	131 Kala
88 Gadha	110 Kunjanikriti	132 Kunda
89 Gaya	111 Swadha	133 Mukunda
90 Nootana	112 Vahini	134 Varada
91 Sumanohari	113 Jalaplava	135 Bhasitha
92 Somavalli	114 Varuni	136 Kandari
93 Somalata	115 Madira	137 Smara
94 Mangala	116 Maitri	138 Preetha
95 Mudrika	117 Haruni	139 Kokilalapa
96 Kshudra	118 Harini	140 Naga
97 Melapaga	119 Maruth	141 Kamini
98 Visvalaya	120 Dhananjaya	142 Kalashodbhava
99 Navaneetha	121 Dhanakari	
100 Nisachari	122 Dhanada	143 Veeraprasoo
101 Nivriti	123 Kachapam	144 Sagaracha
102 Nikadha	124 Kali	145 Satayagna
103 Sara	125 Booja	146 Satavari
104 Samaga	126 Ishani	147 Sragvi
105 Samada	127 Shoolini	148 Patalini
106 Kshama	128 Roudri	149 Pankaja
107 Viswambara	129 Shiva	150 Parameswari

In movable signs, the count is direct and in fixed signs the count is reverse, *i.e.*, the 150th amsa becomes first. In common signs the count is from the 76th amsa. This means the first Nadi Amsa in a common sign will be the 76th in the order given above.

For example, ascendant is Gemini, 16° 40'. As 30° is to 150°, so is 16° 40' to x—the number of passed Nadi Amsas. $x+1$ will be the Nadi Amsa. Hence $x=83$. The Nadi Amsa will be the 84th. Since Gemini is a common sign the count must start from the 76th in the above list. The 84th Nadi Amsa in Gemini will be Sura.

136. General Remarks

We have said above that of all the Shodasavargas, it is the Saptavargas (Art. 109) alone that are of special importance to us as contributing to the positional strength (Sthanabala) of the different planets. The Saptavargas of planets, together with the lord of the Saptavargas, can be tabulated as follows for our future use. Their importance and applicability has been elaborately explained in my book *Graha and Bhava Balas*.

Example 53.—*Tabulate all the Saptavargas af the planets and the Lagna in the Standard Horoscope.*

Table of Saptavargas

Planet	Its Symbol	Rasi	Hora	Drekkana	Saptamsa	Navamsa	Dwadasamsa	Thrimsamsa
Ravi	☉	♎ Sukra	♌ Ravi	♎ Sukra	♎ Sukra	♎ Sukra	♎ Sukra	♏ Kuja
Chandra	☽	♒ Sani	♌ Ravi	♊ Budha	♈ Kuja	♑ Sani	♊ Budha	♃ Guru

Saptavarga Table

Planet	Its Symbol	Rasi	Hora	Drekkana	Saptamsa	Navamsa	Dwadasamsa	Thrimsamsa
Kuja	♂	♏ Kuja	♌ Ravi	♓ Guru	♍ Budha	♐ Guru	♊ Budha	♐ Guru
Budha	☿	♎ Sukra	♌ Ravi	♎ Sukra	♎ Sukra	♎ Sukra	♎ Sukra	♈ Kuja
Guru	♃	♊ Budha	♋ Chan.	♒ Sani	♏ Kuja	♉ Sukra	♓ Guru	♊ Budha
Sukra	♀	♍ Budha	♌ Ravi	♉ Sukra	♋ Chan.	♋ Chan.	♉ Sukra	♑ Sani
Sani	♄	♌ Ravi	♌ Ravi	♌ Ravi	♍ Budha	♒ Sukra	♍ Budha	♈ Kuja
Lagna	Ascdt.	♑ Sani	♌ Ravi	♍ Budha	♑ Sani	♉ Budha	♐ Guru	♍ Kuja

137. Interpretation of Saptavarga Table

Rows horizontal indicate the planets and rows longitudinal—the vargas. Take for instance, the row under the heading Drekkana. Tracing downwards we find the lords of Drekkana occupied by each planet and the names of the Drekkanas. For instance, take the Sun, and tracing horizontally we find under the column Rasi the symbols ♎ and ♀. This means that the Sun is in Thula (Libra) Rasi having Sukra as the lord. The table must be similarly interpreted with reference to other planets.

After thoroughly following this book, you can study *Graha and Bhava Balas*.

Summary

The zodiac is an imaginary band in the heavens extending to 9° on either side of the ecliptic or the path of the Sun. There are 12 signs, each 30°, of the zodiac and 27 constellations, each 13° 20'. The signs (Rasis) and constellations are reckoned from the same point, *viz.*, the first point of Aries.

The planetary system is made up of 9 planets, two of which are the shadowy Rahu and Ketu, the other being the Sun, the Moon, Mars, Mercury, Jupiter and Saturn.

The planets not only revolve round the Sun in orbits but also rotate about their own axis.

All the planets, except the Sun and the Moon, are subject to retrogression and acceleration in their orbits.

The Ayanamsa is the distance between the first point of Aries and the Vernal Point, varying between 19° and 23°. The Sayana school recognises the movable zodiac while the Nirayana school goes by the fixed zodiac.

Rasimana is the time taken for a sign to rise at the horizon and varies from latitude to latitude.

Charakhanda is the ascensional difference, the unit of which is 3 Asu.

Summary

The apparent time of sunrise is the exact moment when the Sun first appears on the eastern horizon of the place. The duration of the day, that is, sunrise to sunset, is called Ahas. Ratri is the duration of time from sunset to sunrise. On the equator Ahas and Ratri are each equal to 30 ghatis or 12 hours. The sum of Ahas and Ratri at any latitude is 24 hours. When the Sun is north of the equator, the day will be longer than the night in duration and *vice versa* when the Sun is south of the equator.

The Equation of Time is the difference between Mean Time and Apparent Time for any moment. This is positive or negative according as the Apparent Time is less or greater than Mean Time.

The Hindu day begins at sunrise and ends with the next sunrise.

1 Day = 60 ghatis = 24 hours
1 hour = 2.5 ghatis

The Sidereal Day is the time taken by the earth to rotate on its axis once with reference to any particular star.

The Solar Day is the time duration between one sunrise and the next sunrise at the same place.

The lunar month or Synodic month has 30 lunar days or tithis and is reckoned from New Moon to New Moon. The solar month is the time taken by the Sun to traverse one sign of the zodiac.

The local mean time varies from longitude to longitude. Longitude divided by 15 will give the local mean time of a place when it is 12 noon at Greenwich.

The standard time is the local time, generally of an important place of a country. Indian Standard Time introduced on 1-1-1906 is 5h. 30m. in advance of Greenwich Mean Time and is calculated for the meridian 82° 30' East.

Suryodayadi Jananakala Ghatikaha is the time duration in ghatis from sunrise to the moment of birth.

The planetary longitudes for any given moment can be calculated by using a standard Panchanga (almanac). Nirayana longitude plus Ayanamsa gives the Sayana longitude of any planet.

The point of the ecliptic at the Eastern horizon at a particular moment is the Lagna or Ascendant for that moment.

The Madhya Lagna is the point at which the ecliptic touches the meridian. It is also called the Dasama Bhava.

The Rasi Chakra is the zodiac with the planets and the Ascendant marked in the various signs. The Bhava Chakra is the division of the heaven into 12 'houses' with reference to time and place.

The duration between midday and the time of day indicated by the Sun's position is *Natha* or meridian distance. *Pragnatha* is the distance between the Sun and meridian when the birth occurs after sunrise or before sunrise. *Paschadnatha* is the distance between the Sun and meridian. When the birth occurs before sunset or after sunset, 30 ghatis minus *Natha* gives *Unnatha*.

Bhava is one-third of the arc intercepted between two adjacent angles. The angles, also called Kendras, are Udaya Lagna (eastern horizon), the Patala Lagna (lower meridian), the Asta Lagna (western horizon), and the Madhya Lagna (upper meridian).

Bhava Sandhi is the point where two Bhavas join. A Bhava is most potent at Bhava Madhya and almost zero at Bhava Sandhi.

Tables of Houses give the sidereal time at birth. Ephemeris or Panchanga provides the planetary longitudes for different days. Sayana longitudes are usually given for Greenwich Mean Time, so that birth time (I.S.T. or L.M.T.) must be converted into G.M.T.

$$G.M.T. = L.M.T. \pm \frac{\text{longitude of place}}{15}$$

+ if place is west of Greenwich
− if place is East of Greenwich.

The Sidereal time of birth is the distance travelled by the Sun from the vernal point.

Each sign of the zodiac can be divided into 16 kinds or vargas. The vargas determine the potency of planets to do good or bad. They are:

1. *Rasi* or sign each being 30°.
2. *Hora* : Each sign is divided into 2 parts of 15° each. The first half is governed by the Sun and

the second half by the Moon in odd signs. In even signs, it is vice versa.

3. *Drekkana* : Each sign is divided into 3 parts of 10° each. The first Drekkana is ruled by the lord of the sign itself, the 2nd by the lord of the 5th therefrom and the 3rd, by the lord of the 9th therefrom.

4. *Chaturthamsa* : Each sign is divided into 4 parts of 7° 30' each. The lord of the first Chaturthamsa is the lord of the sign itself ; that of the 2nd is the lord of the 4th from the sign ; that of the 3rd is the lord of the 7th from it ; and the lord of the 10th is the lord of the 4th Chaturthamsa.

5. *Saptamsa* : Each sign is divided into 7 equal parts of 4° 14' 17 1/7" each. The lords of the first seven signs are the rulers of the Saptamsas of odd signs, while the lords of the 7th and the following signs are lords of the Saptamsas of even signs.

6. *Navamsa* : Each sign is divided into 9 parts of 3° 20' each.

7. *Dasamsa* : Each sign is divided into 10 parts of 3° each. In odd signs the rulers of the Dasamsa are from the sign itself and onwards, while in even signs the rulers of the lords of the 9th and following signs.

8. *Dwadasamsa* : Each sign is divided into 12 equal parts, the lords being the lords of the 12 signs from the sign itself as the first.

9. *Shodasamsa* : Each sign is divided into 16 equal parts. The lords are reckoned from Aries, Leo and Sagittarius for movable, fixed and common signs respectively counted in order.

10. *Vimsamsa* : Each sign is divided into 20 equal parts. The lords of the Vimsamsa are counted from Aries, Sagittarius and Leo for movable, fixed and common signs respectively.

11. *Chaturvimsamsa* : Each sign is divided into 24 equal parts. In odd signs, the rulers are reckoned from Leo onwards. In even signs, the rulers are reckoned from Cancer onwards.

12. *Bhamsa* : Each sign is divided into 27 equal parts. In fiery signs lords of the 27 parts are reckoned from Aries in regular order. In earthy signs, the count is made from Cancer. In airy signs, the counting is from Libra, and in watery signs the rulers are reckoned from Capricorn onwards.

13. *Thrimsamsa* : Each sign is divided into 30 equal parts. In odd signs, the first 5 are governed by Mars, the next 5 by Saturn, the following 8 by Jupiter, the next 7 by Mercury and the remaining 5 by Venus. In even signs, the order is reversed with Venus ruling the first 5, Mercury the next 7 parts and so on.

14. *Khavedamsa* : Each sign is divided into 40 equal parts. In odd signs, the rulers of each part are reckoned from Aries in regular order, repeating

if necessary. In even signs, the counting of rulers of the Khavedamsas begins from Libra.

15. *Akshavedamsa* : Each sign is divided into 45 equal parts. The rulers in movable, fixed and common signs are counted from Aries, Leo and Sagittarius respectively.

16. *Shashtyamsa* : Each sign is divided into 60 equal parts. The longitude of a planet in a sign (without taking into account its longitude as reckoned from 0° of the zodiac) is multiplied by 2. The product is divided by 12. The remainder plus 1 gives the Shashtyamsa Rasi whose lord is its ruler. The product plus 1 counted direct or reverse from the sign according as it is odd or even gives the Shashtyamsa.

17. *Panchamsa* : Each sign is divided into 5 equal parts. In odd signs, the first 5 parts are ruled by Mars, the next 5 by Saturn, the third 5 parts by Jupiter, the fourth 5 by Mercury and the last 5 by Venus. In even signs, the reverse holds good.

18. *Shashtamsa* : Each sign is divided into 6 equal parts. In odd signs, the rulers of the 6 parts are counted from Aries onwards while in even signs, it is from Libra onwards.

19. *Ashtamsa* : Each sign is divided into 8 equal parts. The rulers are reckoned from Aries, Leo and Sagittarius respectively for movable, fixed and common signs.

Summary

20. *Ekadasamsa* : Each sign is divided into 21 equal parts, the lords thereof being reckoned from the 12th from the sign in the anti-clockwise direction.

21. *Nadi Amsa* : Each sign is divided into 150 equal parts, each of 12 minutes of arc. In movable signs, the count is made from the first Nadi Amsa onwards as in the list. In common signs, the count begins from the 76th amsa. In fixed signs, the count starts with the last Nadi Amsa as the first and in reverse.

TABLE I

Charakhandas

Latitude	Vighatis	Vighatis	Vighatis
1°	2.10	1.68	0.73
2	4.20	3.36	1.40
3	6.30	5.04	2.1
4	8.40	6.72	2.8
5	10.50	8.40	3.50
6	12.60	10.08	4.20
7	14.70	11.76	4.90
8	16.90	13.52	5.63
9	19.00	15.20	6.33
10	21.10	16.96	7.06
11	23.30	18.64	7.76
12	25.50	20.40	8.50
13	27.00	21.70	8.80
14	29.90	23.62	9.96
15	32.10	25.68	10.70
16	34.40	27.54	11.46
17	36.60	29.28	12.20
18	39.00	31.20	13.00
19	41.30	33.40	13.76
20	43.70	34.96	14.56
21	46.00	38.00	15.33
22	48.50	80.80	16.26
23	50.90	40.73	16.96
24	53.40	42.72	17.80
25	55.90	44.02	18.63
26	58.50	46.80	19.50
27	61.10	48.88	20.36
28	63.80	50.04	21.26
29	66.50	53.20	22.16

Charakhandas

Latitude	Vighatis	Vighatis	Vighatis
30°	69.30	55.44	23.10
31	72.10	57.68	23.33
32	75.00	60.00	25.00
33	77.90	62.32	25.96
34	80.90	64.72	26.96
35	84.00	67.20	28.00
36	87.10	69.68	29.03
37	90.40	72.32	30.13
38	93.70	74.96	31.23
39	97.20	77.76	32.04
40	100.60	80.48	33.53
41	104.30	83.44	34.73
42	108.00	86.40	36.00
43	111.90	89.52	37.30
44	115.80	92.64	38.60
45	120.00	96.00	40.00
46	124.20	99.36	41.40
47	128.70	102.96	42.90
48	133.30	106.64	44.43
49	138.00	110.40	46.00
50	143.00	114.40	47.66
51	148.20	118.56	49.40
52	153.50	122.83	51.17
53	159.20	127.36	53.06
54	165.20	132.16	55.06
55	171.30	137.04	57.10
56	177.90	142.32	59.30
57	184.60	147.84	61.60
58	192.00	153.60	64.00
59	199.70	159.76	66.56
60	207.80	166.24	69.26

TABLE II

Terrestrial Latitudes and Longitudes

Name of Place	Name of Country	Latitude			Longitude		
Aberdeen	Scotland	57°	10'	N	2°	05'	W
Abyssinia State	Africa	10	00	N	40	00	E
Abu Mount	India	24	40	N	72	45	E
Achin	Sumatra	05	45	N	96	00	E
Aden	Arabia	12	45	N	45	04	E
Adoni	India	15	38	N	77	19	E
Agin Court	France	53	29	N	02	09	E
Agra	India	27	10	N	77	52	E
Ahmedabad	India	23	02	N	72	19	E
Ahmednagar	India	19	01	N	74	52	E
Aix-la-Chapelle	Germany	50	46	N	06	02	E
Ajjaccio	France	41	55	N	08	44	E
Ajmer	India	26	32	N	74	41	E
Ajanta	India	20	31	N	78	19	E
Akyab	Burma	20	18	N	92	45	E
Alleppey	India	09	30	N	76	13	E
Aligarh	India	27	52	N	79	00	E
Alaska	N. America	65	00	N	150	00	E
Alexandria	Egypt	31	12	N	30	10	E
Algiers	N. Africa	36	35	N	25	45	E
Allahabad	India	25	26	N	81	48	E
Almora	India	29	40	N	79	40	E
Alwar	India	27	40	N	77	28	E
Amarapur	Burma	02	50	N	96	02	E
Ambala	India	30	28	N	76	50	E
Amraoti	India (C.P.)	20	56	N	78	00	E
Amraoti	India (Deccan)	16	34	N	80	25	E
Amritsar	India	31	39	N	74	47	E

Latitudes and Longitudes

Name of Place	Name of Country	Latitude			Longitude		
Amsterdam	Netherlands	52°	22'	N	04°	53'	E
Amona	Italy	43	28	N	13	32	E
Ananthapur	India	14	40	N	77	39	E
Andaman (Island)	India	12	00	N	92	45	E
Antwerp	Belgium	51	13	N	04	24	E
Anuradhapura	Ceylon	08	26	N	80	20	E
Arakan	Burma	20	46	N	93	12	E
Arabia (Country)	Asia	24	00	N	48	00	E
Aravali (Hills)	India	26	00	N	74	00	E
Arcot	India	12	55	N	79	20	E
Argentina	S. America	36	00	S	65	00	W
Armenia (State)	Asia	40	30	N	44	30	E
Attock	India	33	55	N	72	20	E
Asia Minor	Asia	30	00	N	32	00	E
Assam (Prov.)	India	20	13	N	75	40	E
Athens	Greece	38	00	N	23	45	E
Atlanta	U.S.A.	33	53	N	84	19	E
Augsburg	Germany	48	18	N	10	53	E
Auarangabad	India	19	53	N	72	22	E
Austria (State)	Europe	47	00	N	14	00	E
Australia		25	00	S	135	00	E
Babylon	Mesopotamia	32	30	N	44	35	E
Bagdad	Mesopotamia	33	29	N	44	31	E
Bahama Is.	West Indies	23	00	N	74	00	W
Baharein Is.	Persian Gulf	26	00	N	50	35	E
Balasore	India	21	31	N	87	00	E
Balsar	India	20	35	N	74	05	E
Baltic Sea	Europe	57	00	N	18	00	E
Baltimore	Ireland	51	28	N	09	19	E
Baltimore	U.S.A.	39	35	N	76	36	W
Baluchistan (State)	Asia	28	04	N	65	00	E

Name of Place	Name of Country	Latitude	Longitude
Banda	India	25° 28' N	80° 22' E
Bangalore	India	13 00 N	77 35 E
Bangkok	Siam	14 00 N	96 15 E
Bareilly	India	28 26 N	79 25 E
Bavanahotte	India	22 18 N	86 10 E
Burdwan	India	23 14 N	87 55 E
Barbados	W. Indies	13 40 N	59 50 W
Baroda	India	22 20 N	73 00 E
Batavia	Java	6 00 N	106 58 E
Bath	England	51 22 N	02 23 W
Bavaria (State)	Germany	48 48 N	12 00 E
Belgaum	India	15 51 N	74 30 E
Belgium (State)	Europe	51 00 N	04 30 E
Belgrade	Yugoslavia	44 57 N	20 37 E
Bellary	India	15 11 N	76 55 E
Belur	India	12 55 N	76 35 E
Banaras	India	25 20 N	83 01 E
Bengal (Prov.)	India	24 00 N	87 30 E
Berar (Prov.)	India	20 35 N	77 00 E
Barbara	(Brit. Somaliland)	10 25 N	46 00 E
Berhampur (Ganjam)	India	19 20 N	84 55 E
Berhampur (Bengal)	India	24 06 N	88 20 E
Bezwada	India	16 40 N	81 00 E
Berlin	Germany	52 31 N	13 24 E
Bethlehem	Palestine	31 41 N	35 15 E
Bhagalpur	India	25 20 N	87 00 E
Bhopal	India	23 15 N	77 23 E
Bhutan (State)	Asia	27 30 N	90 30 E
Bharatpur	India	27 28 N	77 10 E

Latitudes and Longitudes

Name of Place	Name of Country	Latitude	Longitude
Bhuj	India	23° 12' N	68° 02' E
Bikaneer	India	28 00 N	73 22 E
Bidar	India	17 53 N	77 58 E
Bijnour	India	29 26 N	78 10 E
Bijapur	India	16 50 N	75 47 E
Bismark	U.S.A.	46 50 N	100 50 W
Bombay	India	18 54 N	72 49 E
Boordere	India	25 25 N	76 00 E
Boston	England	53 00 N	00 02 W
Brindisi	Italy	40 39 N	17 56 E
Brunswick	Germany	52 15 N	10 22 E
Bucharest	Rumania	44 25 N	26 02 E
Bushire	Persia	29 00 N	50 50 E
Cairo	Egypt	30 02 N	31 40 E
Calais	France	50 57 N	01 51 E
Calcutta	India	22 40 N	88 30 E
Calicut	India	11 15 N	75 51 E
Cambridge	England	52 12 N	00 08 E
Cantebury	England	51 16 N	01 04 E
Canton	China	23 25 N	113 32 E
Cape Town	C. of G. Hope	33 59 S	18 25 E
Chandranagore	India	22 50 N	88 20 E
Cawnpur	India	26 37 N	80 10 E
Charleston	United States	32 54 N	80 00 W
Chicago	United States	41 50 N	87 35 W
Chota Nagpur	India	23 00 N	83 00 E
Cochin	India	09 43 N	76 13 E
Cologne	Germany	50 56 N	06 58 E
Colombo	Ceylon	07 00 N	79 45 E
Constantinople	Turkey	41 01 N	28 55 E
Copenhagen	Denmark	55 40 N	12 34 E
Corsica, I.	France	42 10 N	09 00 E

A Manual of Hindu Astrology

Name of Place	Name of Country	Latitude	Longitude
Costa Rica	Cent. America	10° 00′ N	84° 00′ W
Croydon	England	51 22 N	00 06 W
Croydon	Queensland	18 10 S	142 00 E
Cutch	India	23 30 N	70 00 E
Dacca	India	23 40 N	90 30 E
Dakoth N. St.	U.S.A.	47 00 N	100 00 W
Damascus	Syria	33 33 N	36 18 E
Darjeeling	India	27 05 N	88 06 E
Dartmoor	England	50 38 N	03 58 E
Delhi	India	28 58 N	77 00 E
Derby	England	52 50 N	01 28 W
Devonport	England	50 22 N	04 12 W
Dublin	Ireland	53 23 N	06 15 W
Dunkrik	France	51 03 N	02 26 E
Durban	S. Africa	29 58 S	30 57 E
East London	C. of G. Hope	32 58 S	27 52 E
Ellichpur	India	21 12 N	77 08 E
Emden	Germany	53 22 N	07 13 E
Florence	Italy	43 47 N	11 20 E
Fyzabad	India	26 44 N	82 06 E
Gaya	India	24 45 N	85 05 E
Geneva	Italy	44 25 N	8 59 E
Ghazni	Afghanistan	33 37 N	68 17 E
Gibralter	Spain	36 07 N	05 21 W
Glasgow	Scotland	55 51 N	04 16 W
Goa	India	15 30 N	73 40 E
Golconda	India	17 30 N	78 02 E
Greenwich	England	51 29 N	00 00 E
Gwalior	India	26 22 N	78 02 E
Hague	Netherlands	52 04 N	04 18 E
Halifax	England	53 43 N	01 52 W
Hong-kong	China	22 16 N	114 09 E

Latitudes and Longitudes 163

Name of Place	Name of Country	Latitude			Longitude		
Hyderabad	India	17°	29'	N	78°	30'	E
Hyderabad Sind	Pakistan	25	30	N	68	34	E
Jaipur	India	27	04	N	76	00	E
Jerusalem	Palestine	31	45	N	35	17	E
Jodhpur	India	26	17	N	73	20	E
Jabbulpore	India	23	12	N	79	59	E
Juggennath	India	19	59	N	86	02	E
Kansas City	U.S.A.	39	03	N	94	39	E
Karachi	India	25	00	N	67	03	E
Karaikal	India	11	00	N	79	39	E
Kobe	Japan	35	00	N	135	00	E
Kolhapur	India	16	40	N	74	18	E
Kumbakonam	India	11	00	N	78	40	E
Lahore	India	31	39	N	74	23	E
Lancaster	England	54	03	N	02	28	E
Lashkar	India	26	00	N	77	00	E
Leipzig	Germany	51	20	N	12	21	E
London	England	51	30	N	00	05	W
Los Angeles	U.S.A.	34	20	N	118	45	W
Madras	India	13	04	N	80	14	E
Madrid	Spain	40	25	N	03	40	W
Madura	India	09	50	N	78	15	E
Mahe	India	11	33	N	75	35	E
Mandalay	Burma	22	00	N	96	15	E
Manila	Philippines	14	58	N	121	00	E
Mantua	Italy	45	10	N	10	48	E
Masulipatam	India	16	15	N	81	12	E
Mecca	Arabia	21	20	N	40	20	E
Mascow	Russia	55	40	N	37	40	W
Multan	India	30	12	N	71	31	E
Murshidabad	India	24	02	N	88	00	E
Mysore	India	12	20	N	76	38	E
Naples	Italy	40	52	N	14	13	E

Name of Place	Name of Country	Latitude	Longitude
Natal	South Africa	29° 00' S	30° 30' E
New York	United States	41 00 N	73 55 W
Nilgiri Hills	India	11 15 N	76 30 E
Olympia	Greece	37 40 N	21 20 E
Ottawa	Canada	45 12 N	75 52 W
Paris	France	48 50 N	02 21 E
Poona	India	18 32 N	73 53 E
Puri	India	19 59 N	86 02 E
Quebec	Canada	47 00 N	71 00 W
Quetta	India	30 12 N	67 30 E
Rio de Janeiro	Brazil	22 50 S	43 44 W
Saar, R	Germany	49 28 N	06 45 E
Salt Lake City	U.S.A.	40 55 N	112 00 W
San Francisco	U.S.A.	38 00 N	122 24 W
Seringapatam	India	12 30 N	76 40 E
Shanghai	China	31 28 N	121 28 E
Sheffield	England	53 23 N	01 27 W
Shillong	India	25 31 N	91 58 E
Srinagar	India	34 14 N	74 50 E
Surat	India	21 02 N	72 50 E
Toronto	Italy	40 28 N	17 13 E
Udaipur	India	24 38 N	73 35 E
Waterloo	Belgium	50 44 N	04 23 E

TABLE III

Equation of Time

Date	Jan.	Feb.	March	April	May	June	July	Aug.	Sep.	Oct.	Nov.	Dec.
	M.	M.	M.	M.	M.	M.	M.	M.	M.	M.	M.	M.
1	+3	+14	+13	+4	−3	−2	+3	+6	0	−10	−16	−11
2	4	14	12	4	3	2	4	6	0	10	16	11
3	4	14	12	4	3	2	4	6	−1	11	16	10
4	5	14	12	3	3	2	4	6	1	11	15	10
5	5	14	12	3	3	2	4	6	1	11	16	10
6	6	14	12	3	3	2	4	6	1	12	16	10
7	6	14	12	2	3	1	5	6	1	12	16	9
8	7	14	11	2	4	1	5	6	2	12	16	9
9	7	14	11	2	4	1	5	5	2	13	16	8
10	7	14	11	2	4	1	5	5	3	13	16	7
11	8	14	10	1	4	1	5	5	3	13	16	7
12	8	14	10	1	4	1	5	5	3	13	16	7
13	9	14	10	1	4	0	5	5	4	14	16	7
14	9	13	10	0	4	0	6	5	4	14	16	6
15	9	14	9	0	4	0	6	4	5	14	15	5
16	10	14	9	0	4	0	6	4	5	14	15	5
17	10	14	9	0	4	0	6	4	5	14	15	4
18	10	14	8	0	4	+1	6	4	6	15	15	4
19	11	14	8	1	4	1	6	4	6	15	15	3
20	11	14	8	1	4	1	6	3	6	15	14	3
21	11	14	8	1	4	1	6	3	7	15	14	2
22	12	14	7	1	4	2	6	3	7	15	14	2
23	12	13	7	2	3	2	6	3	7	16	14	1
24	12	13	7	2	3	2	6	2	8	16	13	1
25	12	13	7	2	3	2	6	2	8	16	13	0
26	13	13	6	2	3	2	6	2	8	16	13	0
27	13	13	6	2	3	3	6	2	9	16	13	+1
28	13	13	5	2	3	3	6	1	9	16	12	1
29	13	13	5	3	3	3	6	1	9	16	12	2
30	13		5	3	3	3	6	1	10	16	12	2
31	13		4	3	3	3	6	0	10	16	12	3

TABLE IV

Table of Standard Times

Place	Fast (+) or Slow (−) of Greenwich h. m. s.	Date of Adoption
Aden	+ 3 0 0	Recent
Afghanistan	+ 4 30 0	,,
Africa :		
Cameroons, Fr. Eq. Africa, Tunisia, Angola, Libya,* Nigeria	+ 1 0 0	Sept. 1905
Egypt*, Sudan, Rhodesia, Nysaland, Union of S. Africa, Mozambique	+ 2 0 0	1930
Ethiopia, Kenya, Uganda, Tanganyka, Madagaskar,	+ 3 0 0	Recent
Zanzibar Islands	+ 2 45 0	,,
Algeria*, Morocco, Gold Coast, Ivory Coast, French Sudan, Dahoney*, Togoland, Tangier, Sierra Leone	+ 0 0 0	March 1911
Liberia	− 0 45 0	Recent
Port Guinea, Rio-de-oro*, French Guinea*, Mauretanic*, Senegol*	− 1 0 0	,,
Leopoldville Coquilhatville	+ 1 0 0	,,

* Summer Time observed.

Table of Standard Times

Place	Fast (+) or Slow (−) of Greenwich h. m. s.	Date of Adoption
Africa :		
Orientale, Kivu, Kasai, Ruanda, Urundi, Katanga	+ 2　0　0	Recent
America (U.S.A.) :		
Eastern Time* E.T.‡	− 5　0　0	Nov. 1883
Central Time* C.T.‡	− 6　0　0	,,
Mountain Time* M.T.‡	− 7　0　0	,,
Pacific Time* P. T.‡	− 8　0　0	,,
Alaska :		
Ketchikan to Skagway	− 8　0　0	,,
Skagway to 141° W.	− 9　0　0	,,
141° W. to 162° W.	−10　0　0	,,
162° W. to Western Tip	−11　0　0	,,
America (South) :		
Equator, Columbia, Peru, Territory of Arc	− 5　0　0	,,
Veneezuallah	− 4　30　0	Recent
Western Brazil, Bolivia, Argentina*, Chile*	− 4　0　0	May 1920
British Guiana & Dutch Guiana	− 3　45　0	Recent
French Guiana : Paraguay	− 4　0　0	,,
Uruguay	− 3　30　0	May 1920
Eastern Brazil	− 3　0　0	Recent
Australia :		
Victoria, N.S. Wales, Queensland, Tasmania	+10　0　0	Feb. 1895
South Australia, N. Territory	+ 9　30　0	,,

‡ War time (+ 1 hr.) 9-2-1942 to 30-9-1945.
* Summer Time observed.

168   A Manual of Hindu Astrology

Place	Fast (+) or Slow (−) of Greenwich			Date of Adoption
	h.	m.	s.	
Western Australia	+ 8	0	0	Feb. 1895
New Zealand	+12	0	0	,,
Austria : Hungary	+ 1	0	0	Oct. 1895
Azores*	− 2	0	0	Recent
Ascension Island	0	0	0	,,
Alentian Islands	−11	0	0	,,
Albania	+ 1	0	0	,,
Bahrein Islands*	+ 3	0	0	,,
Belgium*	0	0	0	,,
Bermudas Islands	− 4	0	0	,,
Borneo Islands	+ 8	0	0	Oct. 1904
British Honduras	− 6	0	0	,,
Bulgaria	+ 2	0	0	,,
Burma	+ 6	30	0	1906
Canada :				
Newfoundland	3	30	0	Nov. 1883
Atlantic Time : A.T.*	− 4	0	0	,,
Eastern Time : E.T.*	− 5	0	0	,,
Central Time : C.T.*	− 6	0	0	,,
Canada :				
Mountain Time : M.T.*	− 7	0	0	,,
Pacific Time : P.T.*	− 8	0	0	,,
Canary Islands*	− 1	0	0	Recent
Cape Verde Islands	− 2	0	0	,,
Caroline Islands General	+10	0	0	,,
Kasaie Pinglepag	+10	0	0	,,
Truk	+11	0	0	,,
Ceylon	+ 5	30	0	1906

* Summer Time observed.

Table of Standard Times

Place	Fast (+) or Slow (−) of Greenwich h. m. s.	Date of Adoption
China :		
Kung Lung (Mountain)	+ 5 30 0	Jan. 1903
Sinyang (Tibet)	+ 6 0 0	,,
Lungtsu (Szchuen)* Chung Yuan (Central)	+ 7 0 0	,,
Hong Kong*	+ 8 0 0	,,
Chang Pei (Mountain)	+ 8 30 0	,,
Cocos-Keeling Islands (Indian Ocean)	+ 6 30 0	Recent
Cook Islands (Pac. Ocean)	+10 30 0	,,
Corsica Islands (Med. Sea)*	+ 0 0 0	,,
Costa Rica Islands (Near Panama)	− 6 0 0	,,
Cuba Islands (West Indies)	− 5 0 0	,,
Cyprus Islands (Med. Sea)	− 2 0 0	,,
Czechoslovakia	+ 1 0 0	,,
Denmark	+ 1 0 0	Jan. 1894
Eucador	− 5 0 0	,,
England	0 0 0	1880
Estonia : U.S.S.R.*	+ 2 0 0	Recent
Falkland Islands	− 4 0 0	,,
Fiji Islands	+12 0 0	,,
Finland	+ 2 0 0	May 1921
Formosa*	+ 8 0 0	Jan. 1896
Fernando Islands	− 2 0 0	Recent
France*	0 0 0	May 1911
Gambia	0 0 0	Recent
Germany	+ 1 0 0	April 1892

* Summer Time observed.

170   A Manual of Hindu Astrology

Place	Fast (+) or Slow (−) of Greenwich	Date of Adoption
	h. m. s.	
Gibraltar*	0 0 0	April 1892
Greece and Crete	+ 2 0 0	July 1916
Grenada Islands (W. Indies)	− 4 0 0	Recent
Greenland : Scoresby Sound	− 2 0 0	,,
Angmagssalik, W. Coast excluding Thule	− 3 0 0	,,
Thule	− 4 0 0	,,
Guam Islands	+10 0 0	,,
Guatemala (N. America)	− 6 0 0	1883
Haiti	− 5 0 0	Recent
Hawaiin Islands	−10 0 0	,,
Honduras (Near Panama)	− 6 0 0	,,
Hungary	+ 1 0 0	May 1892
Iceland*	− 1 0 0	Jan. 1906
India : General‡	+ 5 30 0	1-1-1906
Calcutta (L.M.T.)	+ 5 53 0	upto 1-10-1941
Indo-China : Cambodia, Laos, Vietnam	+ 7 0 0	1904
Indonesia : Sumatra (North)	+ 6 30 0	Recent
Sumatra (South)	+ 7 0 0	,,
Java, Borneo (Indonesia)	+ 7 30 0	Recent
Celebes	+ 8 0 0	,,
Molucca Islands	+ 8 30 0	,,
Iraq	+ 3 0 0	,,
Ireland*	+ 0 0 0	Oct. 1915
Israel*	+ 2 0 0	Recent
Italy (and Scicily)	+ 1 0 0	Nov. 1893

* Summer Time observed.

‡ War time (+ 1 hr.) 1-9-1942 to 15-10-1945.

Table of Standard Times

Place	Fast (+) or Slow (−) of Greenwich	Date of Adoption
	h. m. s.	
Japan	+ 9 0 0	1st Jan. 1888
Jordan	+ 2 0 0	Recent
Kamaran Islands	+ 3 0 0	,,
Korean Democratic Republic (North)	+ 8 30 0	,,
Korea (South)*	+ 8 30 0	Dec. 1904
Kuwait (Persian Gulf)	+ 3 0 0	Recent
Latvia* (U.S.S.R.)	+ 2 0 0	,,
Lebanon (Malayan Archi)	+ 2 0 0	,,
Lithuania	+ 1 0 0	,,
Luxemburg	+ 1 0 0	,,
Madagascar	+ 3 0 0	,,
Madeire* (Brazil)	− 1 0 0	,,
Malaya (See footnote)	+ 7 30 0	,,
Malta Islands	+ 1 0 0	,,
Mauritius Islands	+ 4 0 0	,,
Mexico :		
Central Time C.T.	− 6 0 0	Nov. 1883
Mountain Time M.T.	− 7 0 0	,,
Pacific Time P.T.	+ 8 0 0	,,
Marianne Islands	+ 9 0 0	Recent
Marqueass Islands	−10 0 0	,,
Martinique Islands	− 4 0 0	,,
Monaco	0 0 0	,,
Mozambique	+ 2 0 0	,,
Netherlands†	0 0 0	,,
Netherlands Guinea	− 3 40 0	,,

† Summer Time observed.
Malaya: Upto 31-12-1932 : + 7 hrs.
    ,,   31-8-1941 : + 7/20 hrs.
    Now   : + 7/30 hrs.

172   A Manual of Hindu Astrology

Place	Fast (+) or Slow (−) of Greenwich h. m. s.	Date of Adoption
New Caledonia	+ 11 0 0	Recent
Newfoundland	− 3 30 0	,,
New Guinea (British)	+ 10 0 0	April 1911
,, (Netherland)	+ 9 30 0	,,
New Herbrides	+ 11 0 0	Recent
New Zealand	+ 12 0 0	,,
Nicaragua	− 5 45 0	,,
Norfokland	− 11 30 0	,,
Norway	+ 1 0 0	Jan. 1895
Oman	+ 3 30 0	Recent
Pakistan Eastern	+ 5 0 0	Oct. 1951
,, Western	+ 6 0 0	,,
Panama Canal Zone	− 5 0 0	1911
Papua	+ 10 0 0	Recent
Persia	+ 3 30 0	,,
Peseaderes Islands	+ 8 0 0	,,
Philippine Islands	+ 8 0 0	May 1899
Poland†	+ 2 0 0	Sept. 1919
Portugal†	0 0 0	1911
Princess Islands	0 0 0	,,
Puerto Rico	− 4 0 0	,,
Reunion Islands	+ 4 0 0	,,
Roumania	+ 2 0 0	,,
St. Lucia	− 4 0 0	,,
St. Pierre	− 4 0 0	,,
St. Thomas Islands	G.M.T.	,,
St. Vincent Islands	− 4 0 0	,,
Salvador	− 6 0 0	,,

† Summer Time observed.

Table of Standard Times

Place	Fast (+) or Slow (−) of Greenwich h. m. s.	Date of Adoption
Samoan Islands	−11 0 0	1911
Sandwich Islands	G.M.T.	,,
Sarawak	+ 8 0 0	,,
Sardinia	+ 1 0 0	Recent
Saudi Arabia Except Dhahran	+ 3 0 0	,,
Dhahran†	+ 4 0 0	,,
Scotland	G.M.T.	1880
Siam (Thailand)	+ 7 0 0	April 1920
Solomon Islands	+11 0 0	Recent
Somaliland	+ 3 0 0	,,
Serbia	+ 1 0 0	,,
Seychells Islands	+ 4 0 0	,,
Spain†	G.M.T.	Jan. 1901
Spanish Guinea†	G.M.T.	Recent
Society Islands	−10 0 0	,,
Sweden	+ 1 0 0	,,
Switzerland	+ 1 0 0	June 1894
Syria†	+ 2 0 0	Recent
Tahiti	−10 0 0	,,
Tongo (Friendly Islands)	+12 20 0	,,
Tunisia	+ 1 0 0	,,
Tasmania	+10 0 0	,,
Turkey	+ 2 0 0	,,
U.S.S.R. :		
Moscow, Ukrain & West	+ 2 0 0	,,
Black Sea to Caspician Sea†	+ 3 0 0	,,
Sverdlovsk, West Kazak†	+ 4 0 0	,,
Omsk, East Kazak†	+ 5 0 0	,,
Krasnoyarsk, New Syberia†	+ 6 0 0	,,

† Summer Time observed.

A Manual of Hindu Astrology

Place	Fast (+) or Slow (−) of Greenwich h. m. s.	Date of Adoption
U.S.S.R. :		
Irkutsk‡	+ 7 0 0	Recent
Yakutsk, Chitinsk‡	+ 8 0 0	,,
Khabarovsk, Vladivostok‡	+ 9 0 0	,,
Magadan, Sakalin Islands‡	+10 0 0	,,
Peiropavlosvsk, Kamchatsiky‡	+11 0 0	,,
Anadyr	+12 0 0	,,
Vatican Islands	+ 1 0 0	,,
West Indies : Barbados, Guadeloupe, Leeward Isls., Martinique, Tobago, Trinidad, Windward, Isls.	− 4 0 0	,,
Curacao	− 4 30 0	,,
Dominican Republic	− 5 0 0	,,
Bahamas, Jamaica	− 5 0 0	,,
Wales	G.M.T.	1880
Yugoslovakia	+ 1 0 0	Recent
Yokon	− 9 0 0	Aug. 1900

The Summer Time Bill lays down the following rule :—

"The period of Summer Time shall be the period beginning at two o'clock, Greenwich mean time, in the morning of the day next following the THIRD SATURDAY IN APRIL or if that day is Easter Day, the day next following the Second Saturday in April, and ending at two o'clock, Greenwich mean time, in the morning of the day next following the THIRD SATURDAY IN SEPTEMBER."

The Bill will not be permanent but will be renewable annually.

---
‡ Summer Time observed.

TABLE V

Sunrise and Sunset

Latitude Date	0°	10°	20°	30°	35°	40°	45°	50°	55°	60°
January 5	6 1	6 18	6 36	6 57	7 9	7 22	7 38	7 58	8 24	9 1
10	6 4	6 20	6 37	6 57	7 9	7 22	7 38	7 57	8 22	8 56
15	6 6	6 21	6 38	6 57	7 8	7 21	7 36	7 54	8 18	8 50
20	6 7	6 22	6 38	6 56	7 6	7 18	7 32	7 49	8 11	8 42
25	6 9	6 23	6 38	6 54	7 4	7 15	7 28	7 44	8 4	8 32
30	6 10	6 23	6 36	6 52	7 1	7 12	7 24	7 38	7 56	8 21
February 5	6 10	6 22	6 35	6 49	6 57	7 6	7 17	7 30	7 45	8 3
10	6 11	6 21	6 32	6 45	6 52	7 0	7 10	7 22	7 36	7 55
15	6 11	6 20	6 30	6 41	6 47	6 54	7 3	7 13	7 25	7 41
20	6 10	5 19	6 27	6 36	6 42	6 48	6 55	7 4	7 14	7 28
25	6 10	6 17	6 24	6 32	6 36	6 41	6 47	6 54	7 2	7 14
March 1	6 9	6 15	6 21	6 27	6 31	6 35	6 40	6 46	6 53	7 2
5	6 8	6 13	6 18	6 23	6 26	6 29	6 33	6 38	6 43	6 50
10	6 7	6 10	6 14	6 17	6 19	6 21	6 24	6 27	6 30	6 35
15	6 6	6 8	6 9	6 11	6 12	6 14	6 15	6 16	6 18	6 20
20	6 4	6 5	6 5	6 5	6 5	6 5	6 5	6 5	6 5	6 5
25	6 3	6 2	6 1	5 59	5 58	5 57	5 56	5 54	5 52	5 50
30	6 2	5 59	5 56	5 53	5 51	5 49	5 47	5 44	5 40	5 35
April 5	6 0	5 56	5 51	5 46	5 43	5 40	5 35	5 30	5 25	5 17
10	5 58	5 53	5 47	5 41	5 36	5 32	5 26	5 20	5 12	5 2
15	5 57	5 50	5 43	5 34	5 30	5 24	5 17	5 10	5 0	4 47
20	5 56	5 48	5 39	5 29	5 23	5 16	5 9	4 59	4 47	4 32
25	5 55	5 45	5 35	5 24	5 17	5 10	5 0	4 50	4 36	4 18
30	5 54	5 43	5 32	5 19	5 11	5 3	4 52	4 40	4 24	4 4
May 5	5 53	5 42	5 29	5 15	5 6	4 57	4 45	4 31	4 14	3 50
10	5 53	5 40	5 26	5 11	5 1	4 51	4 38	4 23	4 3	3 37
15	5 53	5 39	5 24	5 7	4 57	4 46	4 32	4 16	3 54	3 25
20	5 53	5 38	5 22	5 4	4 54	4 41	4 27	4 9	3 45	3 13
25	5 53	5 38	5 21	5 2	4 50	4 38	4 22	4 3	3 38	3 3
30	5 54	5 38	5 20	5 0	4 48	4 35	4 18	3 58	3 31	2 54
June 5	5 54	5 38	5 20	4 59	4 46	4 32	4 15	3 54	3 25	2 45
10	5 55	5 38	5 20	4 58	4 45	4 31	4 13	3 51	3 22	2 40
15	5 56	5 39	5 20	4 58	4 45	4 30	4 12	3 50	3 20	2 36
20	5 57	5 40	5 21	4 59	4 46	4 31	4 13	3 50	3 19	2 35
25	5 58	5 41	5 22	5 0	4 47	4 32	4 14	3 51	3 21	2 36
30	6 0	5 42	5 23	5 1	4 48	4 34	4 16	3 53	3 23	2 40

LOCAL MEAN TIME

LATITUDE   SUNRISE   NORTHERN

Month	Date	0°	10°	20°	30°	35°	40°	45°	50°	55°	60°
July	5	6 0	5 43	5 25	5 3	4 51	4 36	4 19	3 57	3 28	2 45
	10	6 1	5 45	5 27	5 6	4 53	4 39	4 22	4 1	3 32	2 52
	15	6 2	5 46	5 28	5 8	4 56	4 43	4 26	4 6	3 39	3 1
	20	6 2	5 47	5 30	5 11	5 0	4 46	4 31	4 12	3 46	3 11
	25	6 3	5 48	5 32	5 14	5 3	4 51	4 36	4 18	3 44	3 22
	30	6 3	5 49	5 34	5 17	5 7	4 55	4 42	4 25	4 3	3 33
August	5	6 2	5 50	5 36	5 20	5 11	5 1	4 48	4 33	4 13	3 47
	10	6 2	5 50	5 38	5 24	5 15	5 6	4 54	4 40	4 23	3 59
	15	6 1	5 51	5 40	5 26	5 19	5 10	5 0	4 48	4 32	4 11
	20	6 0	5 51	5 41	5 29	5 23	5 15	5 6	4 55	4 41	4 23
	25	5 59	5 51	5 42	5 32	5 26	5 20	5 12	5 3	4 50	4 35
	30	5 58	5 51	5 44	5 35	5 30	5 24	5 18	5 10	5 0	4 47
September	5	5 56	5 50	5 45	5 38	5 34	5 30	5 25	5 19	5 12	5 2
	10	5 54	5 50	5 46	5 41	5 38	5 35	5 31	5 26	5 20	5 13
	15	5 52	5 50	5 47	5 44	5 42	5 40	5 37	5 34	5 30	5 25
	20	5 50	5 49	5 48	5 46	5 46	5 44	5 48	5 41	5 40	5 37
	25	5 49	5 49	5 49	5 49	5 49	5 49	5 49	5 49	5 49	5 40
	30	5 47	5 49	5 50	5 52	5 53	5 54	5 55	5 57	5 58	6 0
October	5	5 46	5 48	5 52	5 55	5 57	5 59	6 1	6 4	6 8	6 12
	10	5 44	5 48	5 53	5 58	6 1	6 4	6 8	6 12	6 17	6 24
	15	5 43	5 48	5 54	6 1	6 5	6 9	6 14	6 20	6 27	6 36
	20	5 42	5 49	5 56	6 4	6 9	6 14	6 21	6 28	6 37	6 40
	25	5 41	5 50	5 58	6 8	6 14	6 20	6 28	6 36	6 47	7 2
	30	5 40	5 50	6 0	6 12	6 18	6 26	6 34	6 44	6 57	7 14
November	5	5 40	5 51	6 3	6 16	6 24	6 32	6 42	6 54	7 9	7 30
	10	5 40	5 53	6 6	6 20	6 29	6 38	6 49	7 3	7 20	7 42
	15	5 41	5 54	6 8	6 24	6 34	6 44	6 56	7 11	7 30	7 55
	20	5 42	5 56	6 11	6 28	6 38	6 50	7 3	7 19	7 40	8 8
	25	5 43	5 58	6 14	6 33	6 43	6 55	7 9	7 27	7 49	9 20
	30	5 45	6 1	6 18	6 37	6 48	7 1	7 16	7 34	7 57	8 31
December	5	5 47	6 3	6 21	6 41	6 42	7 6	7 21	7 41	8 6	8 42
	10	5 49	6 6	6 24	6 44	6 56	7 10	7 27	7 46	8 13	8 49
	15	5 51	6 8	6 27	6 48	7 0	7 14	7 31	7 51	8 18	8 56
	20	5 54	6 11	6 30	6 51	7 3	7 17	7 34	7 55	8 22	9 1
	25	5 56	6 13	6 32	6 53	7 6	7 20	7 37	7 57	8 24	9 4
	30	5 58	6 16	6 34	6 55	7 8	7 22	7 38	7 59	8 26	9 4

LOCAL MEAN TIME

LATITUDE					SUNSET					NORTHERN

Date	0°	10°	20°	30°	35°	40°	45°	50°	55°	60°
January										
5	18 9	17 52	17 34	17 14	17 2	16 48	16 32	16 12	15 46	15 10
10	18 11	17 55	17 38	17 18	17 6	16 53	16 38	16 18	15 54	15 19
15	18 13	17 57	17 41	17 22	17 11	16 58	16 43	16 25	16 1	15 30
20	18 14	18 0	17 44	17 26	17 16	17 4	16 50	16 33	16 11	15 41
25	18 16	18 2	17 47	17 30	17 21	17 10	16 57	16 41	16 21	15 54
30	18 17	18 4	17 50	17 35	17 26	17 16	17 4	16 49	16 31	16 6
February										
5	18 18	18 6	17 54	17 40	17 32	17 23	17 12	17 0	16 43	16 21
10	18 18	18 8	17 56	17 44	17 37	17 20	17 19	17 8	16 54	16 35
15	18 18	18 8	17 59	17 48	17 42	17 35	17 26	17 17	17 4	16 49
20	18 17	18 10	18 1	17 52	17 47	17 41	17 34	17 25	17 15	17 2
25	18 17	18 10	18 3	17 56	17 51	17 46	17 40	17 34	17 25	17 14
March										
1	18 16	18 10	18 5	17 58	17 55	17 51	17 46	17 40	17 33	17 25
5	18 15	18 11	18 6	18 1	17 58	17 55	17 51	17 47	17 41	17 35
10	18 14	18 11	18 8	18 4	18 2	18 0	17 58	17 55	17 51	17 47
15	18 13	18 11	18 10	18 8	18 7	18 6	18 5	18 3	18 1	18 0
20	18 11	18 11	18 11	18 11	18 11	18 11	18 11	18 11	18 12	18 12
25	18 10	18 11	18 12	18 14	18 15	18 16	18 17	18 19	18 22	18 24
30	18 8	18 11	18 14	18 17	18 19	18 21	18 24	18 27	18 31	18 36
April										
5	18 6	18 10	18 15	18 20	18 24	18 27	18 31	18 36	18 42	18 51
10	18 5	18 10	18 16	18 24	18 28	18 32	18 38	18 44	18 52	19 3
15	18 4	18 10	18 18	18 26	18 32	18 37	18 44	18 52	19 2	19 15
20	18 2	18 11	18 19	18 30	18 36	18 42	18 50	19 0	19 11	19 28
25	18 2	18 11	18 21	18 33	18 40	18 47	18 57	19 8	19 21	19 40
30	18 1	18 11	18 25	18 36	18 44	18 52	19 3	19 15	19 31	19 52
May										
5	18 0	18 12	18 25	18 39	18 48	18 57	19 9	19 23	19 41	20 5
10	18 0	18 13	18 26	18 42	18 52	19 2	19 15	19 30	19 51	20 17
15	18 0	18 14	18 28	18 46	18 56	19 7	19 21	19 38	19 59	20 29
20	18 0	18 15	18 30	18 49	19 0	19 12	19 26	19 44	20 9	20 40
25	18 0	18 16	18 32	18 52	19 3	19 16	19 32	19 51	20 16	20 52
30	18 1	18 17	18 34	18 55	19 7	19 20	19 36	19 57	20 23	21 2
June										
5	18 2	18 18	18 37	18 58	19 10	19 24	19 42	20 3	20 31	21 12
10	18 3	18 20	18 38	19 0	19 13	19 28	19 45	20 7	20 36	21 19
15	18 4	18 21	18 40	19 2	19 15	19 30	19 48	20 10	20 40	21 24
20	18 5	18 23	18 41	19 4	19 17	19 32	19 50	20 12	20 43	21 27
25	18 6	18 24	18 42	19 4	19 18	19 32	19 50	20 13	20 43	21 28
30	18 7	18 24	18 43	19 5	19 18	19 33	19 50	20 13	20 44	21 26

LOCAL MEAN TIME

LATITUDE				SUNSET						NORTHERN
Date	0°	10°	20°	30°	35°	40°	45°	50°	55°	60°

July

Date	0°	10°	20°	30°	35°	40°	45°	50°	55°	60°
5	18 8	18 25	18 43	19 5	19 18	19 32	19 50	20 11	20 40	21 23
10	18 9	18 25	18 43	19 4	19 16	19 31	19 48	20 9	20 36	21 17
15	18 9	18 25	18 43	19 3	19 15	19 28	19 45	20 5	20 31	21 9
20	18 10	18 25	18 42	19 1	19 12	19 25	19 41	20 0	20 25	21 0
25	18 10	18 24	18 40	18 58	19 9	19 21	19 36	19 54	20 17	20 50
30	18 10	18 23	18 38	18 55	19 5	19 17	19 30	19 47	20 9	20 38

August

Date	0°	10°	20°	30°	35°	40°	45°	50°	55°	60°
5	18 9	18 22	18 35	18 51	19 0	19 10	19 23	19 38	19 57	20 23
10	18 9	18 20	18 32	18 47	18 55	19 5	19 16	19 29	19 47	20 10
15	18 8	18 18	18 29	18 42	18 50	18 58	19 8	19 20	19 36	19 56
20	18 7	18 16	18 26	18 37	18 44	18 51	19 0	19 11	19 24	19 48
25	18 6	18 13	18 22	18 32	18 38	18 44	18 52	19 1	19 12	19 22
30	18 4	18 10	18 18	18 26	18 31	18 36	18 43	18 51	19 0	19 13

September

Date	0°	10°	20°	30°	35°	40°	45°	50°	55°	60°
5	18 2	18 7	18 13	18 19	18 23	18 27	18 32	18 38	18 45	18 55
10	18 0	18 4	18 8	18 13	18 16	18 19	18 22	18 27	18 32	18 40
15	17 59	18 1	18 4	18 7	18 9	18 11	18 13	18 16	18 20	18 25
20	17 57	17 58	17 59	18 0	18 1	18 2	18 4	18 5	18 6	18 9
25	17 55	17 55	17 54	17 54	17 54	17 54	17 54	17 54	17 54	17 54
30	17 54	17 52	17 50	17 48	17 47	17 46	17 44	17 43	17 42	17 39

October

Date	0°	10°	20°	30°	35°	40°	45°	50°	55°	60°
5	17 52	17 49	17 46	17 42	17 40	17 38	17 35	17 32	17 28	17 24
10	17 50	17 46	17 41	17 36	17 33	17 30	17 26	17 22	17 16	17 9
15	17 49	17 43	17 37	17 30	17 25	17 22	17 17	17 11	17 4	16 54
20	17 48	17 41	17 34	17 25	17 20	17 15	17 8	17 1	16 52	16 40
25	17 48	17 32	17 30	17 20	17 14	17 8	17 0	16 51	16 40	16 26
30	17 47	17 37	17 27	17 16	17 9	17 2	16 53	16 42	16 29	16 12

November

Date	0°	10°	20°	30°	35°	40°	45°	50°	55°	60°
5	17 47	17 36	17 24	17 11	17 8	16 54	16 44	16 32	16 16	15 56
10	17 48	17 33	17 22	17 7	16 59	16 49	16 38	16 24	16 7	15 44
15	17 48	17 35	17 20	17 4	16 55	16 45	16 32	16 17	15 58	15 33
20	17 49	17 35	17 20	17 2	16 52	16 41	16 28	16 11	15 50	15 22
25	17 51	17 35	17 19	17 1	16 50	16 38	16 24	16 6	15 44	15 13
30	17 52	17 36	17 19	17 0	16 49	16 36	16 21	16 2	15 38	15 5

December

Date	0°	10°	20°	30°	35°	40°	45°	50°	55°	60°
5	17 54	17 38	17 20	17 0	16 48	16 35	16 19	16 0	15 35	14 59
10	17 56	17 39	17 21	17 0	16 48	16 35	16 18	15 58	15 32	14 55
15	17 58	17 41	17 23	17 2	16 50	16 36	16 19	15 58	15 31	14 53
20	18 1	17 44	17 25	17 4	16 51	16 37	16 20	16 0	15 32	14 53
25	18 3	17 46	17 28	17 6	16 54	16 40	16 23	16 2	15 34	14 56
30	18 6	17 49	17 30	17 9	16 57	16 43	16 26	16 6	15 39	15 1

LOCAL MEAN TIME

TABLE VI
Lords of Vargas
LORDS OF RASIS OR SIGNS

No.	Sign	English Names	Symbol	Ruler
1	Mesha	Aries	♈	Kuja
2	Vrishabha	Taurus	♉	Sukra
3	Mithuna	Gemini	♊	Budha
4	Kataka	Cancer	♋	Chandra
5	Simha	Leo	♌	Ravi
6	Kanya	Virgo	♍	Budha
7	Thula	Libra	♎	Sukra
8	Vrischika	Scorpio	♏	Kuja
9	Dhanus	Sagittarius	♐	Guru
10	Makara	Capricorn	♑	Sani
11	Kumbha	Aquarius	♒	Sani
12	Meena	Pisces	♓	Guru

LORDS OF HORA

Hora	1st	2nd
Degrees	15°	30°

No.	Sign	Ruler	Ruler
1	Mesha	Ravi	Chandra
2	Vrishabha	Chandra	Ravi
3	Mithuna	Ravi	Chandra
4	Kataka	Chandra	Ravi
5	Simha	Ravi	Chandra
6	Kanya	Chandra	Ravi
7	Thula	Ravi	Chandra
8	Vrischika	Chandra	Ravi
9	Dhanus	Ravi	Chandra
10	Makara	Chandra	Ravi
11	Kumbha	Ravi	Chandra
12	Meena	Chandra	Ravi

LORDS OF DREKKANA

Drekkana	1st	2nd	3rd
Degrees	10°	20°	30°
No. Sign	Ruler	Ruler	Ruler
1 Mesha	Kuja	Ravi	Guru
2 Vrishabha	Sukra	Budha	Sani
3 Mithuna	Budha	Sukra	Sani
4 Kataka	Chandra	Kuja	Guru
5 Simha	Ravi	Guru	Kuja
6 Kanya	Budha	Sani	Sukra
7 Thula	Sukra	Sani	Budha
8 Vrischika	Kuja	Guru	Chandra
9 Dhanus	Guru	Kuja	Ravi
10 Makara	Sani	Sukra	Budha
11 Kumbha	Sani	Budha	Sukra
12 Meena	Guru	Chandra	Kuja

LORDS OF SAPTHAMSA

Sapthamsa	1st	2nd	3rd	4th	5th	6th	7th
Degrees	4°	8°	12°	17°	21°	25°	30°
Minutes	17'	34'	51'	8'	25'	42'	0'
Seconds	8"	17"	25"	34"	42"	51"	0"
No. Sign			Rulers				
1 Mesha	Ku.	Su.	Bu.	Ch.	Ra.	Bu.	Su.
2 Vrishabha	Ku.	Gu.	Sa.	Sa.	Gu.	Ku.	Su.
3 Mithuna	Bu.	Ch.	Ra.	Bu.	Su.	Ku.	Gu.
4 Kataka	Sa.	Sa.	Gu.	Ku.	Su.	Bu.	Ch.
5 Simha	Ra.	Bu.	Su.	Ku.	Gu.	Sa.	Sa.
6 Kanya	Gu.	Ku.	Su.	Bu.	Ch.	Ra.	Bu.
7 Thula	Su.	Ku.	Gu.	Sa.	Sa.	Gu.	Ku.
8 Vrischika	Su.	Bu.	Ch.	Ra.	Bu.	Su.	Ku.
9 Dhanus	Gu.	Sa.	Sa.	Gu.	Ku.	Su.	Bu.
10 Makara	Ch.	Ra.	Bu.	Su.	Ku.	Gu.	Sa.
11 Kumbha	Sa.	Gu.	Ku.	Su.	Bu.	Ch.	Ra.
12 Meena	Bu.	Su.	Ku.	Gu.	Sa.	Sa.	Gu.

LORDS OF NAVAMSA

Navamsa	1st	2nd	3rd	4th	5th	6th	7th	8th	9th
Degrees	3°	6°	10°	13°	16°	20°	23°	26°	30°
Minutes	20'	40'	0'	20'	40'	0'	20'	40'	0'

No.	Sign				Rulers					
1	Mesha	Ku.	Su.	Bu.	Ch.	Ra.	Bu.	Su.	Ku.	Gu.
2	Vrishabha	Sa.	Sa.	Gu.	Ku.	Su.	Bu.	Ch.	Ra.	Bu.
3	Mithuna	Su.	Ku.	Gu.	Sa.	Sa.	Gu.	Ku.	Su.	Bu.
4	Kataka	Ch.	Ra.	Bu.	Su.	Ku.	Gu.	Sa.	Sa.	Gu.
5	Simha	Ku.	Su.	Bu.	Ch.	Ra.	Bu.	Su.	Ku.	Gu.
6	Kanya	Sa.	Sa.	Gu.	Ku.	Su.	Bu.	Ch.	Ra.	Bu.
7	Thula	Su.	Ku.	Gu.	Sa.	Sa.	Gu.	Ku.	Su.	Bu.
8	Vrischika	Ch.	Ra.	Bu.	Su.	Ku.	Gu.	Sa.	Sa.	Gu.
9	Dhanus	Ku.	Su.	Bu.	Ch.	Ra.	Bu.	Su.	Ku.	Gu.
10	Makara	Sa.	Sa.	Gu.	Ku.	Su.	Bu.	Ch.	Ra.	Bu.
11	Kumbha	Su.	Ku.	Gu.	Sa.	Sa.	Gu.	Ku.	Su.	Bu.
12	Meena	Ch.	Ra.	Bu.	Su.	Ku.	Gu.	Sa.	Su.	Gu.

LORDS OF DASAMSA

Dasamsa	1st	2nd	3rd	4th	5th	6th	7th	8th	9th	10th
Degrees	3°	6°	9°	12°	15°	18°	21°	24°	27°	30°

No.	Sign				Rulers						
1	Mesha	Ku.	Sa.	Bu.	Ch.	Ra.	Bu.	Su.	Ku.	Gu.	Sa.
2	Vrishabha	Sa.	Sa.	Gu.	Ku.	Su.	Bu.	Ch.	Ra.	Bu.	Su.
3	Mithuna	Bu.	Ch.	Ra.	Bu.	Su.	Ku.	Gu.	Sa.	Sa.	Gu.
4	Kataka	Gu.	Ku.	Su.	Bu.	Ch.	Ra.	Bu.	Su.	Ku.	Gu.
5	Simha	Ra.	Bu.	Su.	Ku.	Gu.	Sa.	Sa.	Gu.	Ku.	Su.
6	Kanya	Su.	Bu.	Ch.	Ra.	Bu.	Su.	Ku.	Gu.	Sa.	Sa.
7	Thula	Su.	Ku.	Gu.	Sa.	Sa.	Gu.	Ku.	Su.	Bu.	Ch.
8	Vrischika	Ch.	Ra.	Bu.	Su.	Ku.	Gu.	Sa.	Sa.	Gu.	Ku.
9	Dhanus	Gu.	Sa.	Sa.	Gu.	Ku.	Su.	Bu.	Ch.	Ra.	Bu.
10	Makara	Bu.	Su.	Ku.	Gu.	Sa.	Sa.	Gu.	Ku.	Su.	Bu.
11	Kumbha	Sa.	Gu.	Ku.	Su.	Bu.	Ch.	Ra.	Bu.	Su.	Ku.
12	Meena	Ku.	Gu.	Sa.	Sa.	Gu.	Ku.	Su.	Bu.	Ch.	Ra.

LORDS OF DWADASAMSA

Dwadasamsa	1st	2nd	3rd	4th	5th	6th	7th	8th	9th	10th	11th	12th
Degrees	2°	5°	7°	10°	12°	15°	17°	20°	22°	25°	27°	30°
Minutes	30'	0'	30'	0'	30'	0'	30'	0'	30'	0'	30'	0'

No.	Sign						Rulers						
1	Mesha	Gu.	Su.	Bu.	Ch.	Ra.	Bu.	Su.	Ku.	Gu.	Sa.	Sa.	Gu.
2	Vrishabha	Su.	Bu.	Ch.	Ra.	Bu.	Su.	Ku.	Gu.	Sa.	Sa.	Gu.	Ku.
3	Mithuna	Bu.	Ch.	Ra.	Bu.	Su.	Gu.	Gu.	Sa.	Sa.	Gu.	Ku.	Su.
4	Kataka	Ch.	Ra.	Bu.	Su.	Ku.	Gu.	Sa.	Sa.	Gu.	Ku.	Su.	Bu.
5	Simha	Ra.	Bu.	Su.	Ku.	Gu.	Sa.	Sa.	Gu.	Ku.	Su.	Bu.	Ch.
6	Kanya	Bu.	Su.	Ku.	Gu.	Sa.	Sa.	Gu.	Ku.	Su.	Bu.	Ch	Ra.
7	Thula	Su.	Ku.	Gu.	Sa.	Sa.	Gu.	Ku.	Su.	Bu.	Ch.	Ra.	Bu.
8	Vrischika	Ku.	Gu.	Sa.	Sa.	Gu.	Ku.	Su.	Bu.	Ch.	Ra.	Bu.	Su.
9	Dhanus	Gu.	Sa.	Sa.	Gu.	Ku.	Su.	Bu.	Ch.	Ra.	Bu.	Su.	Ku.
10	Makara	Sa.	Sa.	Gu.	Ku.	Su.	Bu.	Ch.	Ra.	Bu.	Su.	Ku.	Gu.
11	Kumbha	Sa.	Gu.	Ku.	Su.	Bu.	Ch.	Ra.	Bu.	Su.	Ku.	Gu.	Sa.
12	Meena	Gu.	Ku.	Su.	Bu.	Ch.	Ra.	Bu.	Su.	Ku.	Gu.	Sa.	Sa.

Lords of Vargas

LORDS OF SHODASAMSA

Shodasamsa	1st	2nd	3rd	4th	5th	6th	7th	8th	9th	10th	11th	12th	13th	14th	15th	16th
Degrees	1°	3°	5°	7°	9°	11°	13°	15°	16°	18°	20°	22°	24°	26°	28°	30°
Minutes	52'	45'	37'	30'	22'	15'	7'	0'	52'	45'	37'	30'	22'	15'	7'	—
Seconds	30"	—	30"	—	30"	—	30"	0"	30"	—	30"	—	30"	—	30"	—

Rulers

No.	Sign	1st	2nd	3rd	4th	5th	6th	7th	8th	9th	10th	11th	12th	13th	14th	15th	16th
1	Mesha	Ku.	Su.	Bu.	Ch.	Ra.	Bu.	Su.	Ku.	Gu.	Sa.	Sa.	Gu.	Ku.	Su.	Bu.	Ch.
2	Vrishabha	Ra.	Bu.	Su.	Ku.	Gu.	Sa.	Sa.	Gu.	Ku.	Su.	Bu.	Ch.	Ra.	Bu.	Su.	Ku.
3	Mithuna	Gu.	Sa.	Sa.	Gu.	Ku.	Su.	Bu.	Ch.	Ra.	Bu.	Su.	Ku.	Gu.	Sa.	Sa.	Gu.
4	Kataka	Ku.	Su.	Bu.	Ch.	Ra.	Bu.	Ch.	Ku.	Gu.	Sa.	Sa.	Gu.	Ku.	Su.	Bu.	Ch.
5	Simha	Ra.	Bu.	Su.	Ku.	Gu.	Sa.	Sa.	Gu.	Ku.	Su.	Bu.	Ch.	Ra.	Bu.	Su.	Ku.
6	Kanya	Gu.	Sa.	Sa.	Gu.	Ku.	Su.	Bu.	Ch.	Ra.	Bu.	Su.	Ku.	Gu.	Sa.	Sa.	Gu.
7	Thula	Ku.	Su.	Bu.	Ch.	Ra.	Bu.	Su.	Ku.	Gu.	Sa.	Sa.	Gu.	Su.	Bu.	Bu.	Ch.
8	Vrischika	Ra.	Bu.	Su.	Ku.	Gu.	Sa.	Sa.	Gu.	Ku.	Su.	Bu.	Ch.	Ra.	Bu.	Su.	Ku.
9	Dhanus	Gu.	Sa.	Sa.	Gu.	Ku.	Su.	Bu.	Ch.	Ra.	Bu.	Sa.	Ku.	Gu.	Sa.	Sa.	Gu.
10	Makara	Ku.	Su.	Bu.	Ct.	Ra.	Bu.	Su.	Ku.	Gu.	Sa.	Sa.	Gu.	Ku.	Su.	Bu.	Ch.
11	Kumbha	Ra.	Bu.	Su.	Ku.	Gu.	Sa.	Sa.	Bu.	Ku.	Sa.	Sa.	Gu.	Ku.	Su.	Bu.	Ku.
12	Meena	Gu.	Sa.	Sa.	Gu.	Ku.	Su.	Bu.	Ch.	Ra.	Bu.	Sa.	Ku.	Gu.	Sa.	Sa.	Gu.

AN INDEX OF TECHNICAL TERMS

Adi	First
Adhikamasa	Intercalary month
Ahas	Diurnal duration
Akshamsa	Terrestrial Latitude
Angaraka	Mars
Antya	Last
Apamandala	Ecliptic
Apasavya	Sinistral or anti-clockwise
Apoklima	Succeedent house
Aprakashaka grahas	Shadowy planets
Arambha	Beginning
Arambha-sandhi	The starting point
Ashtamsa	$\frac{1}{8}$ division of a sign
Ashuddha Rasi	The sign that cannot be subtracted
Asta	Combustion
Asta Lagna	Descendant
Asu	Equivalent to 4 sec. of Sidereal Time
Athichara	Acceleration
Ayanamsa	Precessional distance
Ayu	Longevity
Ayurbhava	Eighth house
Bhachakra	Zodiac
Bhagana	Revolution of planets
Bhaskaracharya	A Great Hindu Astronomer
Bhava	House
Bhavachakra	Table of House
Bhava-madhya	Mid-point of the house
Bhava-sandhi	Cusp of the house
Bhava-sphuta	Determining longitude of houses
Bhogya	To pass, *e.g.*, time to pass
Bhogyamsa	Arc to gain

Technical Terms Explained

Bhratru	Brother
Bhratrubhava	Third house
Bhuja	Distance from the nearest Equinoctial
Bhuktha	Gained, *e.g.*, Time gained
Bhukthamsas	Arc gained
Bhramana	Planetary rotation
Brihat Jataka	A work on Horoscopy by Varahamihira
Budha	Mercury
Chakra	Diagram, map
Chandra	The Moon
Chandramana	Lunar month
Chara	Variable
Charakhanda	Ascensional difference
Chara Rasis	Movable signs
Chaturthamsa	$\frac{1}{4}$ division of a sign
Dakshina	South
Dakshina Gola	South (celestial) hemisphere; 180° to 360° of the zodiac
Dasamabhava	Mid-heaven
Dasamsa	$\frac{1}{10}$ division of a sign
Dasavargas	The kinds of division, *e.g.*, of a sign
Dhanabhava	Second house
Dhanus	Sagittarius
Dharmabhava	Ninth house
Dhruva	Time of right ascension
Dina	Day, diurnal duration
Dinardha	Half diurnal duration
Drekkana	$\frac{1}{3}$ division of a sign
Dwadasamsa	$\frac{1}{12}$,,
Dwiswabhava Rasis	Common signs
Ekadasamsa	$\frac{1}{11}$ division of a sign
Ghati	Equivalent to 24 minutes of English Time
Gola	Hemisphere
Graha	Planet

Graha Sphuta	Determining planetary longitudes
Guru	Jupiter
Hora	½ division of a sign
Ishtakala	The given time
Jagatchakshu	The Sun
Kalatra	Wife
Kalatrabhava	Seventh house
Kalidasa	A Great Indian Dramatist
Kalpa	4,320,000,000 Sidereal years
Kanya	Virgo
Karaka	Promoter
Karana	Half a lunar day
Karma	Profession
Karma Bhava	Tenth house
Kataka	Cancer
Kendra	Quadrant
Kendra Bhava	Angular house
Ketu	Dragon's tail
Khanda	Division or Section
Kshepa	Celestial Latitude
Kranti	Declination
Kuja	Mars
Kumbha	Aquarius
Kundali	Diagram, map
Labha Bhava	Eleventh house
Lagna	Ascendant
Lagna Sphuta	Longitude of Ascendant
Lipta	A unit of measure of Time or Arc
Madhya	Middle
Madhya Lagna	Mid-heaven
Maharishis	Great Sages of India
Makara	Capricorn
Mandochcha	A celestial force

Technical Terms Explained 187

Mathamaha	Maternal relations
Mathru	Mother
Meena	Pisces
Mesha	Aries
Mithuna	Gemini
Mitra	Friend
Moolatrikonas	Positions similar to those of exaltation
Nadi Amsa	$\frac{1}{150}$ division of a sign
Nadi Vritta	Celestial equator
Naisargika	Natural
Nakshatra	Constellation
Nakshatra Dina	Sidereal day
Natha	Meridian distance
Navamsa	$\frac{1}{9}$ division of a sign
Nirayana	Ex-precession
Oja Rasis	Odd signs
Oochcha	Exaltation
Oopachayas	3, 6, 10 and 11 houses
Pada	Quarter
Panapara	Succeedent house
Panchamsa	$\frac{1}{5}$ division of a sign
Panchanga	Almanac
Panchasiddhantika	A Hindu Astronomical work
Para	A unit of measure of Arc or Time
Paratpara	do.
Paschad	Western
Patha	A celestial force
Pathala Lagna	Lower meridian
Phalit bhaga	Judicial or predictive portion
Pithamaha	Paternal relations
Pithru	Father
Poorvabhaga	Eastern or the first part
Prag	Eastern

Prarupa	A unit of measure of Arc or Time
Prustodaya	Rising by hinder part : *e.g.*, signs
Putra	Son, Children
Putra Bhava	Fifth house
Rahu	Dragon's head
Rasathala Lagna	Lower meridian
Rasi	A zodiacal sign
Rasi chakra	Zodiacal diagram
Rasi mana	Time of oblique ascension
Rasi kundali	Zodiacal diagram
Sama	Neutral
Sandhi	Junctional point
Sani	Saturn
Saptha varga	Seven kinds of division
Satru	Enemy
Satru Bhava	Sixth house
Sauramana	Solar month
Savana Dina	Apparent solar day
Savya	Dextral
Sayana	With Precession
Seeghrochcha	A celestial force
Shadvargas	Six kinds of division
Shashtamsa	$\frac{1}{6}$ division of a sign
Shashtyamsa	$\frac{1}{60}$ division of a sign
Shodasamsa	$\frac{1}{16}$ division of a sign
Simha	Leo
Sirodaya	Rising by the head : *e.g.*, signs
Spashta	Planetary or house longitude
Sthanabala	Positional strength
Sthira Rasis	Fixed signs
Sukha Bhava	Fourth house
Sukra	Venus
Sunya	Zero

Technical Terms Explained

Surya	Sun
Surya Siddhantha	A Hindu Astronomical work
Suryodayadi Janana-kalaghatikaha	Ghatis elapsed from sunrise to birth
Tatkalika	Temporary
Tatpara	A unit of measure of Arc or Time
Thanubhava	First house
Tithi	Luni-Solar day
Trimsamsa	$\frac{1}{30}$ division of a sign
Thula	Libra
Trikona	Trine
Ubhayodaya	Rising both by head and hinder part:
Udaya	Rising [e.g., sign
Udaya Lagna	Ascendant
Unnatha	30 ghatis diminished by Natha
Uttara	North
Uttarabhaga	Second part
Uttara Gola	North (celestial) hemisphere 0° to 180° of the zodiac
Vakra	Retrograde
Varahamihira	A great Indian writer
Varga	Manner of division [Time
Vighati	Equivalent to 24 seconds of English
Viliptha	A unit of measure of Arc or Time
Virama sandhi	End-point
Virupa	A unit of measure of Arc or Time
Vishavarekha	Terrestrial equator
Vrayabhava	Twelfth house
Vrischika	Scorpio
Vrishabha	Taurus
Yugma Rasis	Even signs